DEVELOPMENT AND
UNDERDEVELOPMENT

Development
and
Underdevelopment

 BY CELSO FURTADO

TRANSLATED BY
RICARDO W. DE AGUIAR AND
ERIC CHARLES DRYSDALE

UNIVERSITY OF CALIFORNIA PRESS
Berkeley and Los Angeles   1964

University of California Press, Berkeley and Los Angeles, California

Cambridge University Press, London, England

© *1964 by The Regents of the University of California*

TRANSLATED FROM *Desenvolvimento e subdesenvolvimento*

(RIO DE JANEIRO: EDITÔRA FUNDO DE CULTURA, 1961)

PUBLISHED WITH THE ASSISTANCE OF A GRANT FROM THE ROCKEFELLER
FOUNDATION

Library of Congress Catalog Card Number: 64-19640

Printed in the United States of America

Preface

Development and Underdevelopment brings together a series of studies prepared over a period of almost ten years. The unity of the work comes from the fact that the entire intellectual activity of the author throughout that period has focused on the same goal: to find ways of understanding the ⭠ specific problems of economic underdevelopment.

When the author began more than a decade ago to concern himself with the subject of underdevelopment, the science of economics as taught in the universities in both Europe and the United States provided hardly any points of departure for an approach to this field of study. The theory of prices central to the science of economics was built around the concept of general equilibrium, and any concern for problems of social dynamics was excluded. The student acquired the habit of translating into terms of infinitesimal analysis the basic relationships of economic activity, taking refuge in the rarified atmosphere of high abstractions. From this plane he descended directly to economic geography and the description of institutions. Any insistence upon attention to structural differences gave grounds for suspicion of insufficient assimilation of the scientific method in economics.

Besides the theory of prices and its branches there had emerged, like a volcanic eruption, the elaborate Keynesian construction, whose protracted digestion was still going on in academic circles. For economists reared in the tradition of the theory of equilibrium to try to follow up the surprising trails of Keynesian thought involved intricate mental acrobatics. Nevertheless, the tools of macroeconomic analysis opened up entirely new perspectives and forcefully contributed to breaking through the thick layer of prejudice which had been accumulating under the shadow of an increasingly sterile methodological rigor. However, the neatness of the Keynesian model concealed within its thoroughgoing structure highly suggestive problems which had then only begun to be glimpsed in line with the macroeconomic approach.

The third door open to those who purported to study and understand the world of economic problems was that of Marxian doctrine. This doctrine—to the extent that it reveals the series of irrationalities underlying the contemporaneous social reality and prods creative capacity in the direction of social reconstruction—also helped bring economists into closer contact with the great cultural and human problems of the time. Although Marxism hampered the development of free scientific work in economics, inasmuch as its philosophical postulates, accepted as dogmas, lent a teleological character to economic analysis, it gave rise to an attitude of criticism— almost always constructive in underdeveloped countries, where the persistence of anachronic institutions creates a liability hard to uproot. And since the most urgent and socially most necessary intellectual work in underdeveloped countries was of a critical nature, Marxist thinking reached a high degree of effectiveness, which contributed to its fast penetration during phases of accelerated social change. But as it did not provide constructive solutions outside of dogmatic attitudes, Marxism placed strong limitations on the prospects of creative intellectual effort.

Were we to make a synthesis of the contributions made by these three currents of thought towards the arising of independent and creative economic thinking in the underdeveloped world, we should say that Marxism has spurred the critical and nonconformist approach, whereas the classic economics has served to impose methodological discipline without which analysis swerves toward dogmatism, and the Keynesian outburst has favored a better understanding of the role of the state in economic processes, opening up new vistas in the process of social reform.

The author's evolution in this field has occurred over many years of work as a researcher and analyst, mainly as an economist at the service of the United Nations Economic Committee for Latin America (ECLA). The need for diagnosing the problems of national economic systems in various stages of underdevelopment led him to bring economic analysis closer to the historical method. Comparative study of similar problems on an abstract plane, within variants conditioned by different historical situations and dissimilar national contexts, progressively induced him to adopt a structural view of economic problems. He is convinced that the most necessary effort to be made on the theoretical plane at the present stage consists of the progressive identification of factors that are specific for each structure. That effort will subsequently serve as a basis for establishing a typology of structures. This is, of course, the viewpoint of an economist from an underdeveloped country. It does not exclude the possibility that the theoretical work now being done in developed countries to build up more complete models of typical industrial structures of a more advanced type, within the institutional framework of free enterprise, may continue to play a part in defining concepts and relationships in a very effective manner.

The first chapter of this book outlines the evolution of ideas on development mainly in the English classics, reconstituting the model of development implicit in the most widely accepted economic theory. The author was not concerned with what economists might think about development in general. He asked himself to what point their theories succeeded in "explaining" the process of growth. Those economists who played mainly a critical role, such as the German historical school or the American institutionalists, have been excluded inasmuch as they did not present a systematic interpretation of the process of growth. A first partial rendering of this chapter appeared in Portuguese and Spanish in 1954.[1]

Chapter 2, pertaining to the mechanism of growth, may be taken as an endeavor to identify categories of economic analysis having some universal validity from the point of view of an explanation of the development process. The original text of this chapter was prepared in 1952 as the result of an effort to establish the bases of a technique of economic planning. A partial rendering was published in Portuguese (1952), in Spanish (1953), and in English (1954).[2]

Chapter 3 is an attempt to integrate economic analysis within the historical method in order to explain tentatively the origins of the industrial economy as the basis of modern Western culture. A first rendering of this essay was presented in Portuguese in 1955 and translated into Spanish in 1956.[3]

Chapter 4 opens discussion of the specific problems of underdevelopment; this discussion is expanded in the last two chapters. Together with Chapter 5, it comprises a monograph presented by the author in 1958 for the Department of Political Economy of the Law School of the University of Brazil.

Development and Underdevelopment is addressed to the growing number of persons, mainly of the new generation, who

---

[1] *A Economia Brasileira* (Rio de Janeiro, 1954), Chapter 6, and *El Trimestre Económico,* July-September, 1954.

[2] *Revista Brasileira de Economia,* September, 1952; *El Trimestre Económico,* January-March, 1953; and *International Economic Papers,* No. 4, 1954.

[3] *Econômica Brasileira,* January-March, 1955, and *El Trimestre Económico,* April-June, 1956.

are concerned with problems of underdevelopment. The author is convinced that there is a need for increasing and urgent effort at criticism and reconditioning of economic thought, effort aimed at more effective knowledge of the problems of underdevelopment. In order to contribute to this effort, he presents the following essays—a mere groping along in an almost unexplored field—which may have the merit of suggesting a few points of departure for the preparatory discussion of this constructive work.

C. F.

Recife, February, 1961.

Contents

1 : *The Theory of Development in Economic Science*   1

THE POINT OF VIEW OF THE CLASSICAL SCHOOL :
MARX'S MODEL : THE NEO-CLASSIC APPROACH : THE
THEORY OF THE ENTREPRENEUR : THE THEORY OF
ECONOMIC "MATURITY"

2 : *The Mechanism of Development*   57

THE PROCESS OF DEVELOPMENT : THE RATE OF
DEVELOPMENT

3 : *The Historic Process of Development*   77

AVAILABILITY OF GOODS AND SERVICES : PRODUC-
TION SURPLUS : THE SCHEME OF THE DEVELOPMENT
PROCESS : DEVELOPMENT AS AN EXPANSION OF THE
ECONOMIC UNIVERSE : APPROPRIATION AND THE
SOCIAL ROLE OF THE DOMINANT GROUPS : ASYM-
METRY OF ECONOMIC REGRESSION : EXOGENOUS
FACTORS IN THE DEVELOPMENT OF THE EUROPEAN
COMMERCIAL ECONOMY : TWO SYSTEMS OF PRO-
DUCTION ORGANIZATION IN THE URBAN MERCANTILE
ECONOMY : TENSIONS ON THE LINES OF TRADE; THE
GROWING IMPORTANCE OF THE PROBLEM OF COSTS :
PRODUCTION TECHNIQUES AS A FOCAL POINT OF THE
NEW ECONOMIC SYSTEM : GROWTH AND INSTABILITY
AS INHERENT FACTORS OF THE FREE ENTERPRISE
INDUSTRIAL ECONOMY

4 : *Elements of a Theory of Underdevelopment*   115
   THE CLASSIC MODEL OF INDUSTRIAL DEVELOPMENT :
   THE UNDERDEVELOPED STRUCTURES

5 : *External Disequilibrium in Underdeveloped
   Structures*   141
   STRUCTURAL CAUSES OF DISEQUILIBRIUM : CURRENT
   MONETARY ANALYSIS OF THE PROBLEM OF DISEQUI-
   LIBRIUM : A REFORMULATION OF THE PROBLEM

Index   173

1 : *The Theory of Development in Economic Science*

The theory of economic development endeavors to explain, from a macroeconomic point of view, the causes and mechanism of the persistent growth in productivity of the labor factor and the repercussions of this growth on the organization of production and on the distribution and utilization of the social product. That explanatory task is projected here on two planes. The first, in which abstract formulations prevail, comprises analysis of the actual mechanism of the process of growth. This investigation calls for building models or simplified schemes of existing economic systems, models based on stable relationships between calculable variables deemed to be relevant and important. The second, the historical plane, comprises critical study in the light of a given reality and on the basis of categories defined by the abstract analysis. It is not enough to construct an abstract model and provide an explanation of how it operates; it is just as important to demonstrate the explanatory effectiveness of such a model as applied to historic realities. Only the latter procedure can reveal the limitations inherent in the level of abstraction at which the model is drawn up and suggest what changes must be introduced in order to make it valid from the point of view of a given reality.

The stable relationships (of a functional or causal-genetic type) with which the economist works are derived not directly from the observation of the real world but from more-or-less simplified schemes of reality. Hence the fundamental methodological problem facing the economist is that of defining the level of generality (or specificity) at which any relationship becomes valid; that is, to what extent is it possible to eliminate from a given abstract model simplifying assumptions incompatible with the historic reality under consideration without invalidating the model's explanatory efficacy. Such a methodological problem acquires special importance in the field of development theory for two main reasons. The first is that it is impossible in this area of study either to eliminate the time factor or to ignore the irreversibility of the historic economic processes. This impossibility makes it hard to arrive at any generalization on the basis of the observations on record for a given moment. The second reason is that it is likewise impossible to ignore the structural differences of economies in different stages of development. The aforementioned relationships presuppose some structural stability; it is, then, a twofold problem that faces us: to ascertain to what extent it is possible to generalize in regard to other structures observations on record for another structure, and to define relationships which may be deemed sufficiently general to retain their validity in the course of some structural changes. What explanatory value might a model have if it is general enough to meet those requirements? The accuracy of economic analysis consists precisely of defining the limits of such validity. The effort to reach higher levels of abstraction must be accompanied by another effort aimed at defining in terms of historical realities the limits of validity of the relationships inferred. The fundamental double nature of economic science —its character at once abstract and historical—thus comes out to the full in the theory of economic development.

That economics has up to the present time been considered a purely abstract science is due to the fact that at the time of

Ricardo its purpose was almost totally limited to the study of the distribution of the product. When the economic process is viewed from the standpoint of the distribution of income flow, some categories are at once identified which, owing to their generality, do permit analysis at a high level of abstraction. Such broad generalization may lead the analyst to attribute a universal validity to the theories he formulates, albeit the basis of his observations may be extremely limited. Let us take as an example the Ricardian theory of rent. The relative scarcity and diversity of arable land are observations which, though made in one county, in England, show every sign of being universally applicable. By considering the rent phenomenon as deriving from those two factors, Ricardo might well expect that his theory might be universally applicable. But neither can the relative scarcity of land be presented as a universal prototype nor can the forms of production organization be ignored when the distribution of the social product is being studied.

An economist observing economic processes not from an exclusively distributive viewpoint but primarily as a production system must come down to the historical plane, and this compels him to be more cautious in his generalizations. Ricardo can provide us a further example. It is known that Ricardo had no interest in problems connected with production and explicitly viewed them as outside the field of economics. Yet in the third edition of his *Principles* he included a chapter on the study of the repercussions on the organization of production due to introduction of the use of machines. Then he appropriately stated that generalizations on the basis of English experience were not to be applied to other countries (which we would today call underdeveloped) in which the relative availability of productive factors was different from that in Britain.[1]

The question of the abstract or historical nature of the

---

[1] D. Ricardo, *On the Principles of Political Economy and Taxation,* Chapter 31 (included in *Works*).

method used by the economist is not, then, independent of the problems concerning him. Economic development is a phenomenon with clear-cut historical aspects. Each economy in the course of development faces a cluster of problems specific to itself, although many of them individually may be common to other contemporaneous economies. The complex of natural resources, the migratory currents, the institutional order, and the relative degree of development of the dominant contemporaneous economies singles out each historical phenomenon of development. Let us take Cuba as an example. Few economies have developed faster than Cuba's, thanks to her growing integration into international trade. However, few are today facing greater difficulties in emerging from stagnation due to the nature of the relationships of external interchange. Thus foreign trade appears as both a stimulating and a restrictive factor in relation to development.[2]

No less antiscientific, however, would be the position of an economist limiting himself to a mere description of historic cases of development. Had he not available an adequate analytical tool, he would never succeed in understanding, for instance, the role played by fluctuations in the external demand for sugar in the process of capital formation of the Cuban economy. And such a tool would not exist at all had economic science not reached some degree of universality pertaining to the definitions of broad basic concepts whose explanatory validity, though limited, has undeniable practical bearing. It is because we are often forgetful of the limitations of that validity when approaching problems in concrete historic situations that we pass surreptitiously from the field of scientific speculation into that of dogma. The "great laws" of the classic economists included, for example, "free competition" and "free exchange." Both consisted, in the ultimate analysis, of logical constructions based on fragmentary observations, on simplistic

---

2 Written in 1954.

psychological assumptions, on a given social structure, and on relations between expanding economies and others of a relatively stagnant type. Nevertheless, by dint of sheer repetition these formulations became transformed into dogma. As a result, economics for a long time lost the features of an objective science and became a mere collection of precepts.[3] Hence continuing criticism of economic thought by economists themselves is a prerequisite of the advancement of this science.

THE POINT OF VIEW OF THE CLASSICAL SCHOOL

As we have mentioned above, the increase in productivity of labor and its repercussions on the distribution and utilization of the social product comprise the central problems dealt with by the theory of development. Yet pertinent interest lies not in some productivity increase in this or that enterprise in itself. To be sure, there can be no productivity increase in the economy as a whole except, generally speaking, through improvements in individual enterprises; but it would be a mistake to infer a theory of development from a specific study of those enterprises or of the mechanisms of single markets.[4]

Increased economic productivity at the enterprise level sometimes reflects only an increase in the entrepreneur's prof-

---

[3] "We are only too well aware that throughout the past century economists, speaking in the name of their science, have been airing views on what they considered to be socially imperative. They have proceeded to calculate, *immediately on the basis of their findings,* the course of action which is economically 'desirable' or 'right,' just as they have also opposed certain policies on the ground that their realization would decrease the general 'welfare' or imply the 'neglect' (or even the 'infringement') of economic laws. Even when the claim is not explicitly expressed, the conclusions unmistakably imply the notion that economic analysis is capable of yielding laws in the sense of *norms and not merely laws in the sense of demonstrable recurrences and regularities of actual and possible events.*" Gunnar Myrdal, *The Political Element in the Development of Economic Theory* (London, 1953), p. 4.

[4] See on page 80 (original) or 54 (translation), the Keynesian criticism of the neoclassical viewpoint on this matter.

its, without any effects on the aggregate income. Hence productivity increases on the microeconomic plane must not be mixed up with development, which can hardly be conceived of without a rise in the real income per capita. Nevertheless, the increased physical productivity at the enterprise level, because it often involves a labor-saving factor, has much bearing on the mechanism of development.

Theory of Production

If social productivity is defined as the total product per unit of occupied time of the working force of a community, the theory of development becomes mainly a macroeconomic theory of production. It is thus that the theory of development can be fitted into general economic theory. When formulating the theory of long-term variations in aggregate production, economists would therefore be furnishing the bases for a theory of economic development. Let us see to what extent that latter theory has been effectively formulated.

What can be expected of a theory of production? That it tell how the process of production has been undergoing changes, historically speaking; that it make clear the causes of changes in production levels as well as the functional and causal relationships between production growth and the form of income distribution, and between the changes in the latter and the rate of accumulation; finally, that it state what would be the maximum feasible rate of accumulation and under what conditions this might be reached, either in free-enterprise economies or in economies with a central control of the use of production factors.

By and large, economists have been not only systematically unconcerned with problems pertaining to the productive process but have even sometimes stated explicitly that those problems are not encompassed by the purposes of economic science.[5] In Adam Smith the study of production, although

---

[5] See Edwin Cannan, *History of the Theories of Production and*

dealt with in unequal fashion, does take up quite some space. He was concerned with the problem of *why* the social product grows. (This interest almost disappeared from the treatises of later English economists.) Smith ascribes the cause of the phenomenon to the division of labor, to which he attributes three virtues: an increase in dexterity, a saving of time, and the possibility of the use of machines. But after such a felicitous start, Smith's analysis suddenly falls to a lower level: he states that the division of labor is the result of "a certain propensity in human nature to truck, barter, and exchange one thing for another," and that the size of the market limits the division of labor. We thus fall into a vicious circle: the size of the market depends upon the productivity level and the latter upon the division of labor, which, in turn, depends upon the size of the market.[6]

The classics of the first half of the nineteenth century, following the lead of J. B. Say, classified the "elements of production" under three major headings: land, capital, and labor. Nevertheless, they ascribed to labor the origin of all "value," the social product being the resultant of the amount of labor utilized, both directly and indirectly. However, the amount of labor which could be used was determined by the amount of capital accumulated. This theory implicitly laid it down that the level of real wages was not arbitrary—and therefore could not be changed by the action of either labor unions or the government—but was dependent upon the labor supply and the employment capacity of the economy. And employment capacity was seen as a function of the accumulation of capital.[7] Despite its limited aim, the scope that such a theory

---

Distribution in English Political Economy from 1776-1848, 3d ed. (London, 1924).

[6] Adam Smith, *An Inquiry into the Nature and Causes of the Wealth of Nations.* Edited by Edwin Cannan. See Chapters 1, 2, and 3.

[7] More accurately, it was a function of the "wage fund," which amounted to the available circulating capital.

could have as an explanation of the historical process of production growth was considerable.

But the economists of the first half of the nineteenth century—at least in England—saw in the process of capital accumulation not the key to a theory of growth but the proof that the development then on record was a fleeting phenomenon. Their reasoning was caught between the "pincers" of the Malthusian "principle of population" and the "law of diminishing returns" which was supposed to prevail in farming. Those pincers had a clear ideological foundation, the one side pointing to the theory of wages, the other to the theory of rent. Ricardo, the great ideologist of the British industrial class, argued that rent tended to increase whenever low-quality land was utilized. On the other hand, according to the principle of Malthus, the population tended to grow whenever workers' wages rose above the subsistence level. When the land-population ratio was favorable, as in recently settled countries, both wages and profits were high. The rate of accumulation had to be large and farm income low. High wages, however, promoted fast growth of population and the use of low-quality land. With increasing prices of foodstuffs, the cost of manpower would rise, as would rent. Hence the overall productivity of the employed population would tend to fall, while rent would rise. Wages would decline to the subsistence level and profits tend to disappear. With this model, Ricardo established two principles of much practical scope. The first was that the rise of wages presupposed capital accumulation and was not to be carried out at the cost of the entrepreneurs' profits; the second held that the landowner class tended to become a growing social burden which could be reduced only through a policy of free imports of agricultural products.

Based on such polemical arguments, developed by the economists of the British industrial class in the heat of the struggle against the landowners and a working class then becoming

organized, J. S. Mill developed his famous "general theory of
the economical progress," which is really a theory of the
tendency towards the stationary state.[8]

Mill fittingly asked what role technical progress plays in the
economic process. As he saw it, such progress delays the advent
of the stationary state but cannot avoid it, since the pressure
towards falling profits is ever greater. Ricardo, with more
practical sense, knew how to use the argument of technical
progress for polemical purposes. "With every increase of capital and population, [the price of] food will generally rise,"
Ricardo says, "on account of its being more difficult to produce. The consequence of a rise of food [prices] will be a
rise of wages, and every rise of wages will have a tendency
to determine [capture] the saved capital in a greater proportion than before the employment of machinery. Machinery
and labour are in constant competition, and the former can
frequently not be employed until labour [cost] rises."[9] Hence
technical advancement would be the means of defense of the
capitalist class against rising wages. The rise in wages does not
benefit the workmen, however, but those who draw income
from the land. In this view, then, the working class was
crushed between the capitalists, who could defend themselves
with technical progress, and the landowners, who profited
from a particularly antisocial monopoly. Thus Ricardo sum-
moned all social forces against the main enemy of the industrial class—the landowners. In that argument the idea of a
trend towards stagnation was nevertheless also implicit.

Ricardo also admits that technical progress in some particular instances might increase the net product to such an extent
that all classes, including the working class, would reap benefits. Yet the classical economists, generally speaking, saw
technical progress more than anything else as means of replac-

---

[8] John Stuart Mill, *Principles of Political Economy* (London, 1895),
pp. 494-498.

[9] Ricardo, *op. cit.*

ing manpower by capital. Adam Smith's subtlety in ascribing the increase in productivity to the division of labor, while ignoring the effects upon the latter of the greater density of capital per person employed, created verbal difficulties almost unsurmountable by his followers. If the increase in productivity was due to the division of labor, this increase would be ascribed to labor and not to capital. Accumulation of capital was merely a requirement of the division of labor.[10]

Undoubtedly the classical economists seem always, when building their models, to have in mind economies in the course of development. In Adam Smith that idea of development emerges explicitly and in dogmatic form. Economic progress would seem to be a natural phenomenon, occurring in "almost all nations . . . even in those who have not enjoyed the most prudent and parsimonious governments."[11] Yet that idea of economic progress is not accompanied in Smith by an explanation that could integrate it within the broader body of economic science. Although he discusses extensively the accumulation of capital, he restricts himself to an external description of the process, without grasping its connections with technical progress and productivity increases. Smith's successors, as we have seen, were led by polemical considerations to approach the problem of capital accumulation from the viewpoint of the theory of distribution.[12] They were interested in knowing whether the levels of rent and of wages would tend to rise or

---

[10] Adam Smith felt the accumulation of circulating capital preceded the division of labor (*op. cit.*, Vol. I, p. 258), but the division of labor was the stimulus to the use of fixed capital, chiefly machines (*ibid.*, p. 395). Anyhow, he does not seem to admit that technical improvement might be capable of increasing labor productivity without previous capital accumulation: "It is by means of an additional capital only that the undertaker of any work can either provide his workmen with better machinery, or make a more proper distribution of employment among them" (*ibid.*).

[11] *Ibid.*, p. 326.

[12] In the Preface to his *Principles,* Ricardo affirms that the "main problem of political economy" is "to determine the laws which regulate" distribution.

not, in relative terms, as a result of capital accumulation. Thus the latter process was transformed into a datum whose causal connections were of small concern.

Finally, J. S. Mill, endeavoring to reformulate the theory of production development by means of tools and concepts hammered out in the heat of discussions on distribution, has supplied us with that major absurdity, under the guise of a theory of "economical progress," which tells us only that there can be no progress at all. He did recognize that the economy of his time was growing, but in order to be coherent with his own premises he insinuated that stagnation may be inevitable. Indeed, he provided an extremely vague statement opening the door for any way out whatsoever: ". . . if we had not reached it [stagnation] long ago, it is because the goal itself flies before us."[13] And for what reason? Here is the most surprising element of the whole picture: because technical development and the export of capital were modifying the terms of the problem. Had J. S. Mill initially reasoned in terms of production he would not have constructed his model while ignoring the most dynamic of all elements belonging to it— namely, technical advancement. He would surely have perceived that the most important thing was to explain why the terms of the problem were undergoing changes. But he limited himself to carrying through to its ultimate consequences the argument with which Ricardo tried to demonstrate that the prime mover of social progress, profit, is permanently threatened in its operations by the rising costs of manpower, either in arbitrary rises in wages or rises in rents due to protectionist policies.

MARX'S MODEL

The position of Marx in the development of the ideas that have shaped economic science may be presented as a special

---

[13] Mill, *op. cit.*, p. 495.

case, susceptible of contradictory interpretations. The following comments have the limited purpose of surveying his contribution—that is, defining the scope of the model he has constructed as an explanatory element of the developmental process of the capitalist economy.

At the outset it must be borne in mind that Marx started his economic analysis from a philosophical approach to history. To be sure, the classical economists were not devoid of a philosophy of history. But none of those so far mentioned used economic analysis primarily as a tool in laying the foundations of a theory of history. Marx did this for the first time, and this approach was to lend extraordinary penetrative force to his ideas. The enormous influence he has exerted is not due to any great contribution of his theories to major progress in the development of economic analysis in his time; nor is it that his own philosophy of history (and its implicit message) constituted great advancement within the movement of socialist ideas of the nineteenth century. His impact stems from his having reasoned out—with the tools of analysis of the only social science that had then reached some degree of methodological precision—a set of philosophical concepts which did correspond, and still do correspond, to the continuing yearnings for a lasting renewing of the modern culture that emerged from the industrial revolution.

Marx tells us in an oft-quoted text how his philosophical thinking had led him into economic analysis.[14] Hegel's philosophy of law induced him to meditate upon the causes which determine the forms of the state and the juridical relations between citizens. How to explain those facts on the basis of a mere hypothesis pertaining to the general evolution of the human mind? To the extent that he meditated upon this, he became aware that "the anatomy of . . . society is to be sought

---

[14] Karl Marx, *A Contribution to the Critique of Political Economy*, translated from second German ed. by N. I. Stone (Chicago, 1904), p. 11.

in political economy." He finally reached the conclusion—
which was to become the definitive philosophical basis of his
work—that the production of mankind's means of sustenance
is a social fact from which various necessary relationships of
production are derived, and that those relationships correspond to the development of productive powers. All Marx's
subsequent efforts on the economic plane were to be matters
of identifying the fundamental production relations in the
capitalist regime and of determining the factors acting towards
the development of the productive powers, the factors which
lead to the superseding of that regime. One must not lose
sight of those ultimate aims, for the whole of Marx's economic
thinking may be taken as an effort in that direction.

We have noted earlier that the thinking of the English
classics had assumed an "actuating" form which might to some
extent be considered revolutionary. Actually, the classicists had
adopted a sharply critical attitude with regard to the residues
of the feudal society which, at the time they wrote, were
benumbing the full development of the forces of capitalism.
As a consequence of his philosophical attitude, Marx was to
assume, with regard to the whole of the political institutions of
his time, a position almost unique among economists of the
second half of the nineteenth century. Imbued with Hegelian
dialectics, which he defined as the science of the general laws
of movement of both the external world and human thinking,
he observed capitalism not only from the standpoint of the
factors which hampered its development, but chiefly from that
of its overall dynamics, "inner contradictions," historical dimensions, beginning and end. The classicists had reasoned in
backward-turning evolutive terms, as if the institutional framework of capitalism represented the crowning stage of human
evolution. Marx, in ascribing an ideological foundation to that
position, tried to demonstrate the historical meaning of
capitalistic institutions. To sum up, the position of the classics
may be described as ideological-revolutionary, the rationali-

zation, as it were, of forces tending to consolidate a historical situation in full course of advancement. Marx's position, on the other hand, could be called utopian-revolutionary, a rationalization of forces tending to overcome a historical situation already consolidated.

Production Relationships and the Theory of Surplus Value

Let us see how Marx used classical economic analysis to lay the foundations of his concept of history, establishing thereby a basis for a theory of political action. We have pointed out that at the heart of his concern lay the problem of production relationships. He soon realized the scope afforded by the classical economists' labor theory of value for the analysis of production relations in the capitalistic regime. The classicists had utilized it as a tool for developing an elementary theory of prices. Marx saw in it something far more important: the grounds for his theory of surplus value which, ultimately, is the "anatomy" of the class struggle in the capitalist regime.

The law of value or the theory of labor value in the classical economics had, according to Myrdal, "its origin in the natural law doctrine that labour is the legal ground of property."[15] For Adam Smith that doctrine served as a foundation for a theory of prices holding it to be more-or-less obvious that two things requiring the same amount of time to manufacture should have the same value and be sold for approximately equal prices. In a handicraft-farming type of economy this reasoning had much validity. Smith, as we have seen, contributed to the consolidation of this way of viewing the problem of "value" by overestimating the effects of the division of labor, to which he ascribed every increase in productivity. One must not forget that in Smith's day capital was nothing but a reserve of consumption goods, whose period of rotation was very short. The increase of that reserve would cause the number of persons employed outside the subsistence economy to increase

---

[15] Myrdal, *op. cit.*, p. 80.

too, resulting in a larger aggregate product. The classical economists continued to think about capital in terms of a "wage fund," in spite of the vast subsequent development of fixed capital in the productive processes. Marx, however, largely refuted this anachronistic view.[16]

The law of value, a mere point of departure for a theory of relative prices in a pre-capitalist economy, in Marx's hands acquires quite another kind of importance. In the first place, he reasons in abstract and macroeconomic terms. He defines labor as the entire working capacity of a community. His concept of the value of each good is that it is the materialization of a portion of that "abstract labor." Independent of the price such good may fetch on the market, its *value*—insofar as the community is concerned—is expressed by that portion of abstract labor. Yet that abstract labor does not float in the air, but exists as an aspect of the "labor force" of working people. The labor force is a merchandise that is sold and bought on the market, a merchandise that has the inherent quality of carrying the abstract labor implicit within itself. Marx makes use of the Aristotelian-Smithian dichotomy of use-value and exchange-value to explain that phenomenon. The use-value of labor is the value-creating capacity of the abstract labor; labor's exchange-value is the market price of the labor force, that is, workmen's wages. A far-reaching distinction is involved. As a matter of fact, if the capacity for creating value is limited to labor and its price is wages, it could be inferred that the total value of goods is expressed by their cost in wages. Marx's distinction is aimed at making it clear beyond a doubt that value is generated by that portion of "socially necessary" abstract labor embodied in the good and in no way corresponds to the labor force factor sold by the workman to his employer in line with the market conditions.

---

[16] See, in particular, *Capital*, Vol. I, Chapter 24, Sec. 5. All quotations from that work are taken from the English edition prepared under the direction of Engels and reprinted in Moscow, 1954.

Let us now see the true scope of the dichotomy between labor (understood as abstract labor, that is, the whole working capacity of a community) and the labor force. From the macroeconomic viewpoint, labor is evidently the source of the social product—that is to say, the amount of value which a community produces within a given time period. The community being conceived of as a whole, the level of technology, the available natural resources, and the equipment brought together may be considered as data. Labor becomes the sole production factor, and it may be affirmed that the level of production will be determined by the amount of labor utilized. Having reasoned at such a level of abstraction, Marx proceeds to argue in terms of the individual worker, whose labor force he considers to be the source of the entire mass of social work. In other words, there is only one manifestation of socially useful labor, namely, the labor force of the wage earner. He infers from this that the productive capacity of a community is the sum of the labor forces of the wage earners. Everything that is not wage labor is ignored as not having any capacity for generating value. Hence it is enough that one compare the net social product with the mass of wages paid in its production in order to define the social surplus or "surplus value" which corresponds to the fruits of the "unpaid labor" of the workers.

Marx's theory of value has been widely criticized since the time of Böhm-Bawerk. Although those criticisms may seem crushing, their effects upon the followers of the theory have been insignificant. The fact of the matter is that more often than not such criticisms have been aimed at secondary targets. Critics have always started with the idea that a theory of value cannot have any aim other than that of serving as a basis for a theory of relative prices. It is easy to demonstrate that the Marxian theory of value is of limited scope as a basis for a theory of relative prices.[17] But what Marx aimed at was not to

[17] In Volume III of his *Capital,* Marx develops his price theory on

establish the relative prices of commodities, but to formulate the bases for a theory of surplus value.

Marx's transition from the macroeconomic plane (mass of social labor) to the microeconomic (individual work) has quite different implications when the analysis shifts from the static to the dynamic. In fact, "for a determined lapse of time" the available resources, state of the arts, and accumulated capital may be admitted as data, by reasoning as if there were but a single production factor, labor. If, however, we make a comparison between two distinct time periods, the problem acquires quite another aspect: to go on reasoning in terms of a single factor forces us to ascribe every productivity increase to that single factor. In maintaining that position Marx was compelled to ignore the time factor in the productive process; he did this by reasoning in microeconomic terms. He refuted the classic concept that saving constitutes a sacrifice and demonstrated that it is merely a result of the large concentration of resources in a few hands. Saving ensures to the capitalists their monopoly of production goods and arms them to acquire ownership of a larger portion of the social product. Such an argument does make sense on the microeconomic plane, of course—but not altogether on the macroeconomic level. Whatever the form of appropriation of the social product may be, if a part of it is not saved there will be no productivity increase. It may be asserted that this saving is the "unpaid labor" of the worker; in any case, it cannot be ignored that without such saving there can be no productivity increase. At the microeconomic level, Marx argued in strictly moral terms, pointing out that the "sacrifice" involved in saving is made by the workers exclusively, and in order to avoid contradictions on the macroeconomic level he arbitrarily established a difference between the product resulting from

the basis of "productive prices," which include an "average rate of profit." This theory was implicitly stated in Volume I, as will be seen later.

labor and that deriving from the productivity increase. The former was invested with value, the latter was not.

Labor, according to Marx, is not only the sole source of value but also has the quality of "transmitting to its products the value of the means of production embodied in them."[18] Thus for Marx the labor concept became highly abstract, independent of space and time. He even states that an English and a Chinese weaver working the same number of hours "create equal values."[19] On the other hand, he declares: "Though the same quantity of labour adds always to its products only the same sum of new value, still the old capital-value, transmitted by labour to the products, increases with the growing productivity of labour."[20] With such an argument he tries to negate completely the idea that capital may have any capacity whatsoever of creating value. Technical progress affords the laborer control of larger quantities of equipment, raw materials, etc., and the possibility of producing more per unit of resources utilized. The product per unit of utilized labor increases, but the value *directly* generated by labor cannot increase. To sustain that argument it is necessary to assume that the value of the physical unit of the product tends to decline to the extent that the physical productivity of labor increases as a result of technical progress. In this logic, the concept of value becomes extremely ambiguous and its use begins to raise serious obstructions in Marx's economic analysis.

Although he does not make his own theory of relative prices immediately explicit, Marx utilizes it to explain the price of the labor force, without which he could not manage to round out the surplus value theory. In fact, the difference between the "value" of the labor force of the worker and its value-

---

[18] *Ibid.*, Vol. I, p. 605.
[19] *Ibid.* This concept is untenable, for "abstract labor," being of a social nature, cannot be the same in both England and China.
[20] *Ibid.*

creating capacity is the element that defines the magnitude of the surplus value. He reasons that the value of the labor force is given by its "production price"—the price of the commodities necessary for the maintenance and reproduction of the worker. (This formulation of a price theory, implicit in the theory of surplus value, was developed by Marx only at a much later stage.) Market prices tend to be fixed not in terms of value but of price of production. The former computation reflects the rate of the surplus value,[21] whereas the latter computation is made on the basis of an average profit rate. Yet production price is only the price of supply. Factors acting on the side of demand are able to make it rise or fall. Depending upon the conditions in the labor market, the price of the labor force may be either higher or lower and the mass of the surplus value is larger or smaller. For a given society it is possible to establish the maximum of surplus value which the capitalists are able to extract within a given period of time. That maximum is expressed by the physiological subsistence wage. Marx noted that under the conditions of his day wages were above that level, for they contained a historical component embodied in the psychological minimum.

With this elaborate theory of surplus value Marx intended to lay a scientific foundation for his doctrine of class struggle. By asserting that production has a social character—that is, that the sole creative source of value is the social labor applied in each activity in line with prevailing techniques—and by contending that the appropriation of the product is of a private nature inasmuch as the labor force is sold as a commodity to the owner of the production instruments, he thought he had identified the basic production relationship of the capitalist system. Those who produce are precluded from profiting from the full fruits of their efforts; they are compelled to content themselves with negotiating their work with those

---

[21] Ratio between unpaid and paid labor, as explained more fully below.

who hold the monopoly of the instruments of production. The two groups are thus in profound antipathy. The clash of these antagonistic interests comprises the prime mover for the development of the productive forces.

The Theory of Accumulation and Development of Productive Forces

Deeper exploration of Marxian analysis, from the standpoint of the theory of development, requires defining his basic concepts more fully. In Marx, the value of the social product is expressed as the sum of three variables: constant capital (C), variable capital (V), and surplus value (S). Constant capital comprises the depreciation of equipment, consumed raw materials, fuels; variable capital involves wages paid; and surplus value is the difference between the sum of C + V and the market value of product obtained—that is, the product's cash equivalent. The ratio $i = S/V$, the rate of surplus value, constitutes the portion of the net product remaining in the hands of the capitalist; Marx also calls this factor the "degree of exploitation." The ratio $j = V/C$, the organic composition of capital, indicates what portion of the latter can generate new value. Another important relationship in Marx's analysis is the profit rate: $r = S/(C + V)$. From the standpoint of the individual capitalist the surplus value rate (S/V) is of little concern. What does interest him is the relationship between what he has earned and the total capital invested $(C + V)$. On the other hand, the profit rate also depends on the speed of turnover of capital (K). Hence we can define the profit rate as

$$r = \frac{iV}{K(C + V)}.$$

In the subsequent analysis these three relationships (i, j, and r) are critical.

It was stated above that the aims of the Marxian analysis were to define the production relationships of the capitalistic economy (doctrine of class struggle) and to ascertain the factors that spur the development of production forces in a capitalistic regime. Let us now take up this second aspect of the problem.

At first sight the analysis of the development of production forces seems to be mixed up with the theory of development. As a matter of fact, Marx's own philosophical attitude, concerned with the "laws of movement," seems to corroborate such a conclusion. Yet it must be pointed out that his interest lies more in the search for "the law for the setting in motion of the capitalist system" than in the ongoing development of an economic system. We shall see that, according to his analysis, the capitalistic system is on the move precisely because it is developing. Its development, however, consists of creating adequate conditions for its own displacement, such conditions being due to growing internal contradictions. In other words, it is a development with growing disequilibria, tending to a cataclysmic disruption in which the regime will be submerged. This is a philosophical concept derived from the combination made by Marx of Hegelian dialectics with the French socialist doctrines he had absorbed in his youth. Out of the great exertions Marx made to provide this philosophical concept with a foundation emerged his theory of capitalistic accumulation. He seemed to realize that it was possible to formulate a broader theory of economic development,[22] but narrowed his attention down to the specific case of "movement of the capitalistic society."

For his analysis of the operation of the whole economic system, Marx conceived a very simple but extremely elucidative model. He divided the economy into two departments:

---

[22] See *op. cit.*, p. 598, for example.

(1) that making production goods and (2) that making consumption goods. Describing the production of each of these departments in terms of the three above-mentioned variables we have:

$$(1) = C_1 + V_1 + S_1$$
$$(2) = C_2 + V_2 + S_2.$$

He then considered a first hypothesis in which there would be no net investment (simple reproduction). In this case the total production value of department 1 is intended for capital replacement in the two departments. Thus: $C_1 + V_1 + S_1 = C_1 + C_2$. Whence: $C_2 = V_1 + S_1$. In this situation, production of consumption goods must exceed the consumption of persons connected with this production (either workers or capitalists) to the extent that it is necessary to provide sustenance for people meeting the needs of replacement of equipment. This model of simple reproduction may be easily rendered dynamic if we distribute S between capitalists' consumption and capital.[23] This gives a relatively wider aspect to department 1. The surplus of consumption goods in department 2 will therefore tend to grow.[24]

The significance of this model resides in its showing that the accumulation process is not the result of arbitrary decisions but of historical factors expressed by the production structure itself. "The use that can be made of the total annual product," says Marx, "depends entirely upon its own composition . . . ."[25] "In one word, surplus value is convertible into capital solely because the surplus product, whose value it is, already comprises the material elements of new capital."[26]

On the other hand, the model also indicates, in the case of the broadened reproduction, that the surplus product corre-

---

[23] Marx uses the word capital with the threefold meaning of appropriation of surplus product, savings, and investment.

[24] This model is developed in *Capital,* Vol. II, Chapters 20 and 21.

[25] *Ibid.,* Vol. I, p. 580.

[26] *Ibid.,* p. 581.

sponding to S has the twofold aim of providing for the capitalists' consumption and for their wish to increase their capital, to accumulate. Marx does not indicate clearly what principles preside over the distribution of the surplus between the capitalists' consumption and accumulation. Presumably he construed a stable ratio between them when, on the one hand, he states that it is inherent in the dynamics of the regime that capitalists be engaged in undertaking new investment, inasmuch as competition tends to expel those lagging behind. On the other hand, Marx also states that consumption apparently tends to grow with the expansion of the surplus and to become institutionalized at new levels.[27]

Accumulation is not so much a consequence of the appropriation of surplus by the capitalist class as of the way in which surplus is distributed among its members. Indeed, the development of capitalism takes the form of a permanent change in the organic composition of the aggregate capital of the community. When productivity rises, with technical progress, the amount of equipment per employed worker also increases. In other words, constant capital (C) grows more quickly than variable capital (V). For the community as a whole, as we have already seen, this merely implies, in the Marxian view, that the physical volume of the product tends to grow faster than the value of the product. Nevertheless, the situation appears in a different guise for the individual capitalist. By intensifying accumulation and incorporating new techniques, he reduces the cost of his own production. Until competition corrects this state of affairs, the capitalist enjoys a relative increase in the surplus value, which is manifest in an increased rate of profit. Inasmuch as the diffusion of new techniques is carried out through these individual advances, the total

---

[27] "When a certain stage of development has been reached, a conventional degree of prodigality, which is also an exhibition of wealth and consequently a source of credit, becomes a business necessity to the 'unfortunate' capitalist." *Ibid.*, p. 594.

quantity of surplus value is distributed unequally among the capitalists, which creates an atmosphere of permanent conflict between them. The result of this conflict is the elimination of the weaker and a tendency to growing concentration of capital in the hands of a few.

Summarizing what we have covered so far, we may state that the rise in surplus value is due to historic factors connected with the minimum level of subsistence of the working class and to factors acting on a short-term basis which are connected with the defensive capacity of the workers and the aggressiveness of the capitalist class. Marx leaves this issue entirely open and sharply criticizes the point of view of the classics (the wage fund law), according to which it was impossible for the workers to improve their standard of living by forcing a rise in monetary wages. Given a rate of surplus value it is important to consider how the surplus is distributed by the capitalists between their own consumption and the formation of new capital.[28] In this case, too, Marx would appear to ascribe great importance to historical factors, as a result of which there would be a certain amount of stability in this distribution. What decides the amount of new investment is mainly the total mass of surplus value. The rate of savings is merely a result of the clash between the desire of the capitalist class to consume and the "need" on the part of each individual capitalist to accumulate so as to avoid being excluded by competitors. This need on the part of the capitalists to force accumulation leads them to seek to increase their participation in the product—that is, their rate of profit. This action on the part of the individual capitalist has two significant connections.

---

28 The distribution of surplus value among the various forms of capital, industrial profit, commercial profit, rent, interest, etc., is not of major interest from the point of view of the theory of accumulation. Marx considers the capitalists *as a class* and attaches little significance to conflicts between the members of that class. However, he does present an interesting theory of absolute and differential rent. See especially *ibid.*, Vol. III, Part 2, Chapter 47.

On the one hand, as we have seen, there is intensified competition between the capitalists, exerting pressure towards greater accumulation. On the macroeconomic level, it is translated in pressure to increase the rate of surplus value. To be sure, an individual capitalist can increase his rate of profit by merely adding to the relative surplus value. The capitalists as a whole can do it, however, only if there is an increase in the entire surplus, that is, the absolute surplus value of the community. Marx considers that each capitalist struggles permanently to increase his own absolute surplus value, obliging the workers to work longer hours, or managing to pay less through recruitment of women and children. But there is a limit to what can be achieved in this respect. The temporary gain in the relative surplus value is an automatic consequence of the way in which new techniques are acquired through accumulation.

Hence the basic role in the accumulative process is played by the capitalist.[29] His consumption would appear to be a function of the volume of the surplus. This, in turn, is determined by the aggressiveness with which the capitalists endeavor to increase absolute surplus value. The volume of investment, on the other hand, is a function of the surplus and of the penetration of new techniques, for it is these latter that permit the increase in the relative surplus value and stir up competition among the capitalists. Although the rate of surplus value derives from the action of the capitalist class as such (that is, from the fact that the production goods are the private property of a small minority), the dynamism of the system, in the ultimate analysis, emerges from the distribution of the surplus value through competition among capitalists individually. And in that competition the introduction of new techniques is the main weapon of attack of one against the others. Hence in the evolution of capitalism the tendency to

---

[29] "Fanatically bent on making value expand itself, he ruthlessly forces the human race to produce for production's sake." *Ibid.*, Vol. I, p. 592.

concentration of ownership necessarily accompanies the accumulative process.

Marx does not present his model precisely as we have expressed it, inasmuch as he has very little interest in emphasizing possible contradictions within the capitalist class. He encounters the prime mover of the capitalistic economy in the class struggle, the philosophical postulate from which he started and which was the cornerstone of his theory of political action. That is why he ascribes tremendous importance to the antagonism between capitalists and wage-earners, the former striving to increase the rate of surplus value and the latter struggling to achieve minimum subsistence conditions. Thus the analysis he makes of the dynamics of the system is intended not to describe the forces which guide its development but to demonstrate that its internal contradictions tend to become intensified. Having reached the conclusion that the fundamental tendency is towards accumulation, he then inquires what is the influence of the growth of capital on that part of the product which comes into the hands of the working classes.[30] In other words, how is the tendency towards accumulation reflected in the "fundamental contradiction" and how is this tendency translated in terms of class struggle? There is thus an imperceptible progression from the economic analysis itself to the corroboration of a philosophical concept on the basis of particular elements of this analysis. In this progression, however, important elements foreign to the initial model are introduced, as we shall now see.

The process of accumulation is studied first of all from the point of view of the changes it causes in the organic composition of the capital. The most important factor to be considered in this analysis, says Marx, "is the composition of the capital and the changes it undergoes in the course of the process of accumulation."[31] We have seen that the social

[30] *Ibid.*, p. 612.
[31] *Ibid.*

product consists of the constant capital (C) (depreciation of equipment, raw materials, fuels), variable capital (V) (wages), and surplus value (S). We have also seen that the ratio V/C is defined as the organic composition of the capital. This organic composition varies from branch to branch of industry and often from company to company within a single branch. Inasmuch as V is the only value-creating source, it is easy to deduce that the ratio of quantity of value created to total quantity of capital invested varies according to the organic composition of the capital. If, therefore, with the process of accumulation, investments in constant capital increase more than those in variable capital, the organic composition of the capital is modified. From the point of view of a single company, the problem, as we have seen, is a simple one: what it produces has less value, but, as the price in the market is fixed, it can increase its relative surplus value. From the macro-economic point of view, however, there is another problem. If we suppose that the rate of surplus value (S/V) remains constant, we implicitly assume that real wages tend to increase. On the other hand, if it is predicated that real wages are stable, we must conclude that the rate of surplus value tends to increase. Now the rise in the rate of surplus value necessarily causes a rise in the average rate of profit, unless the duration of capital turnover is reduced, that is, unless capital becomes under-utilized. As we have seen, the rate of profit (r) depends on the rate of surplus value (i) and turn-over of capital (K):

$$r = \frac{iV}{K(C+V)}.$$

Let us see now how Marx carries out his analysis, starting from the evidence (which he considers to be a currently observed fact) that the organic composition of capital tends to undergo modification in the sense of a relative increase in constant capital. Right from the start he recognized that the increase in C with regard to V should be reflected in an intensification in the demand for labor. Other factors being constant, larger investment in machinery, buildings and so on obviously implies greater demand for workers. The bargaining position of the latter improves, prompting a tendency to rising wages: "The demand for laborers may exceed the supply, and, therefore, wages may rise."[32] Marx nevertheless considers that this tendency cannot go on for long, inasmuch as the decline in the rate of profit diminishes the rate of accumulation, with a consequent reduction in the demand for labor. This is a temporary movement and "the mechanism of the process of capitalist production removes the very obstacles which it temporarily creates."[33]

He then introduces into argument the progress of techniques, "the most powerful lever of accumulation."[34] Marx sees in technological progress the basic instrument used by the capitalistic class to increase the labor supply. So powerful is that instrument that, notwithstanding the tendency already indicated towards increased demand for labor, "a disposable industrial reserve army" exists permanently in any capitalistic economy. This reserve army, belatedly introduced into the model, comes to play a fundamental role in it. Apparently Marx starts out from the observation, current in his day and repeatedly mentioned in the whole of the literature referring to the "industrial revolution," that the labor supply is wholly elastic. The penetration of techniques into farming shifts into the cities a growing sector of population. On the other hand, the handicrafts sector, in a state of disorganization, swells up the army of the urban underemployed. However, in spite of being a matter of current observation, a large permanent surplus of labor can be integrated into the model only in rather arbitrary fashion. The fact of the matter is that the unemploy-

---

32 *Ibid.*, p. 613.
33 *Ibid.*, p. 619.
34 *Ibid.*, p. 621.

ment was due to the disaggregation of the pre-capitalistic economy and ought therefore to be considered as corresponding
to one phase of capitalistic evolution. To incorporate it into
the model, Marx would first have had to demonstrate that
unemployment was inherent in the capitalist regime itself, and
a consequence of its internal contradictions. Only thus could it
be conceded that such unemployment would tend to become
intensified. The industrial reserve army arose as an external
element introduced into the model so as to make it possible
to affirm that, with the accumulation and progress of technique, there would be growing pressure to reduce wages.
"The greater the social wealth," states Marx, "the greater is
the industrial reserve army." He called this *"the absolute general law of capitalist accumulation."*[35]

Marx could therefore conclude that the basic fact of the
dynamics of capitalism is that the increase in wealth necessarily implies an increase in the number of those who do not
have access to work. Hence the causes of class struggle increase with the growth in the wealth of the community. It
might be deduced from this circumstance that the situation
of the capitalist class would constantly improve as a result
of the pressure on wages exerted by the industrial reserve
army. This, however, was not exactly the way it turned out.
We have already seen how, on a long-term basis, accumulation—making C grow by comparison with V—exerts pressure
towards a decline in the rate of profit. It was assumed to be an
unquestioned truth in the classic economics that on a long-
term basis the rate of profit tended to decline. We have seen
the somber conclusions drawn by J. S. Mill from this fallacy.
Deduced from the "population principle" of Malthus and the
law of differential rent of Ricardo, it went on to demonstrate
that any attempt at an arbitrary increase in real wages would
be to no practical purpose. Marx perceived the role of this

---

[35] *Ibid.*, p. 644 (italics from Marx's text).

idea in demonstrating the temporary nature of capitalism. As a matter of fact, if the rate of profit tends to decline down to nothing, that is tantamount to saying that capitalists as a class tend to disappear. This argument, sketched out in the first volume of *Capital*, was thoroughly developed only in the third volume.[36] Marx there presents an extremely simple argument. Making V equal to 100, he ascribes to C the following values: 50, 100, 200, 300, and 400. The rate of surplus value (100 per cent) he makes constant; it appears as 100 in every case. Thus the rate of profit declines from $66\frac{2}{3}$ per cent in the first case $100/(50 + 100)$ to 20 per cent in the last $100/(400 + 100)$. In this manner, Marx seeks to establish on a new basis the theory of the tendency to a decline in the profit rate, making it independent of the rough "population principle."

In their struggle to avoid the decline in the rate of profit, the capitalists would avail themselves of every possible means, especially (a) more intensive exploitation of the labor forces, (b) export of capital, especially to the colonies (an idea which was later to be developed by Lenin in his thesis on imperialism), and (c) intensification in accumulation so as to augment the absolute quantity of the mass of profit. Marx attaches especial attention to the third argument. As a matter of fact, with an increase in the mass of employed workers and concentration of capital in constantly reduced number of hands, it can readily be deduced that a falling rate of profit might coincide with a growing absolute quantity of profit in the hands of the capitalists. But it was nonetheless true that, if the rate of profit went on declining permanently, a moment would arrive when the system would tend to undergo a catastrophe and enter into a state of complete collapse. Marx believed that cyclical crises were forerunners of such collapses. These crises, by raising unemployment and forcing a decline in wages, and by furthermore eliminating the marginal capi-

---

[36] *Ibid.*, Vol. III, Chapters 13-15.

talists and facilitating concentration of wealth, make it possible to improve matters and regain normality; but by no means do they modify the long-range tendencies. The successive crises would inevitably lead to the final breakdown of the system, with the elimination of the capitalist class, which would by then be merely dead weight in the productive forces.

Thus, in his concern with demonstrating that the capitalistic system was fated to disappear—without ever daring to prognosticate whether the final crisis would occur in ten or in a hundred years—Marx endeavored to prove far more than was possible with the tools of analysis available to him. Actually, as we have already indicated, the concept of a decline in the rate of profit presupposes increasing idleness of capital or a reduction in the rate of surplus value—that is, an increase in the participation of wage earners in the product. As the net product is distributed between wage earners (V) and capitalists (S), reducing the part of the capitalists must be increase that of the wage earners. But this would be in sharp disagreement with Marx's *absolute general law of capitalist accumulation* [Marx's italics], according to which the industrial reserve army keeps the wage earners permanently on the defensive.

In his eagerness to brace his philosophical ideas with economic arguments, Marx utilized the instruments of economic analysis too broadly. Following the line of reasoning of the classics and using current observation, he declared that constant capital tends to increase more intensively than variable capital—that is, the supply of labor. If no attention is paid to the progress of techniques, there are grounds for deducing from this argument that the rate of profit tends to decrease. J. S. Mill went that far. But accumulation of capital cannot be disassociated from the progress of techniques, which has the contrary effect inasmuch as it permits the replacement of labor by capital. Mill understood that these two forces might cancel each other, but he assumed that, while accumulation was a perennial process, the advancement of techniques would be

an occasional one. Marx, on the other hand, realized that the
progress of techniques was a factor whose effects went far
beyond those of accumulation itself. He therefore concluded
that, no matter how intensive accumulation might be, the
supply of labor would be more and more elastic, taking the
form of growing technological unemployment. Ricardo, however, had already realized that techniques must be "economical" if they are to be utilized. In other words, new machinery
is purchased only when its price is favorable in comparison
with that of the labor that is saved. Hence there is an interde-
pendency between the assimilation of new techniques and the
price of labor. Marx gives a good example of that interdependence when he mentions the case of farming in England between 1849 and 1859. At that time there was a rise in the level
of real wages of the farm worker. And as a result more
machinery was introduced "and in a moment the laborers
were redundant again in a proportion satisfactory even to the
farmers."[37] It must not be forgotten that both accumulation
and assimilation of new techniques are due to the initiative
of the capitalist. As Marx himself states, "the independent
variable is the rate of accumulation." The capitalist needs,
above all, to accumulate. In his act of accumulation, however,
he improves the bargaining position of the worker; but he then
counterattacks with new techniques tending to reduce the
demand for labor. The extent to which these two factors do
or do not compensate one another can be observed empirically.
What is indeed without any basis in logic is the assumption
that the rate of profit may decline without increased participation by wage earners in the product.[38]

---

[37] *Ibid.*, Vol. I, p. 638.

[38] For the model as presented by Marx to have any logical consistency,
it would have to be assumed that effective demand was persistently
inadequate. In that case, however, the rate of investment would rapidly
tend to decline to nothing. The argument might be used as a component
of a theory of crises, but not to explain long-term tendencies. Even so,
the causes of this persistent insufficiency of effective demand would need
explaining.

Marx endeavored to demonstrate through the concept of the industrial reserve army that it is in the interest of the capitalists to maintain part of the labor force permanently unemployed. But if it is true that this arrangement keeps wages relatively low, it is also true that the capitalists would fail to appropriate the large quantity of value which might be created by the unemployed. Inasmuch as the great challenge to the capitalist is to invest his new capital (even more so if the concept of a permanent decline in the profit rate of capital already invested is accepted), it might then be asked how it is possible for technological unemployment to increase continually. It would not be easy to reconcile such unemployment with the existence of idle capital. Furthermore, we have to start from the principle that the whole of the capital is being used reproductively and that technological unemployment is due to the fact that techniques are advancing faster than accumulation. In view of this, there would have to be a substantial increase in productivity. Hence it would be fitting to consider two hypotheses: in the first, real wages remain stable and the rate of surplus value increases—the capitalists would have their hands full of new capital which would necessarily lead to progressive absorption of previously unemployed labor; in the second, real wages increase and the rate of surplus value remains constant or declines. But an increase in real wages is incompatible with the existence of a great mass of unemployment. Hence the idea of Marx that capitalism may advance with increasing unemployment, at the cost of greater and greater advances in techniques, lacks logical consistency.

The way in which Marx presents his model leads one to suppose that the persons most interested in the destruction of capitalism are the capitalists themselves. Actually, there is no contradiction between the maintenance of the surplus value rate—that is, the "degree of exploitation of the wage earner by the capitalist"—and an increase in real wages. Furthermore, as the development of capitalism is carried out with concentration of capital, the mass of the surplus in the hands of each capitalist may grow faster than the net product without it being necessary to reduce participation by wage earners in that product; a change in the rate of surplus value need not occur. If, as is a matter of everyday observation, the constant capital of the community grows faster than the population, it is understandable that there should be a tendency to increased participation by wage earners in the net product. But, inasmuch as accumulation is inseparable from the progress of technique and the orientation of technology is provided by the capitalists, it is similarly understandable that the latter should endeavor to correct that tendency. When they do not succeed in doing so, the "opportunities" for new investments decline and the reduction in the rate of accumulation curtails the rise in real wages. If they succeed only too well, they create technological unemployment but increase the quantity of resources available for new investments. The latter, if effected, will create new employment opportunities and absorb the surplus. Leaving out of consideration the phenomena resulting from insufficiency of effective demand, which did not enter into Marx's long-range approach, there is nothing to indicate any inherent tendency in the capitalist system to cumulative modification in the distribution of the net product between wage earners and capitalists. To discover such a tendency Marx introduced into his model an extrinsic factor: the industrial reserve army. Not trusting the results, however, he subsequently came back to the classic notion of the long-term tendency to a decline in the rate of profit, but placed it on totally inconsistent bases.

Historic experience, showing that the development of capitalism takes place with growing real wages and without a marked change in the distribution of the net product between wage earners and capitalists, proved Marx was by no means correct in endeavoring to base his philosophical ideas on economic analysis. This does not necessarily mean that his

concept of capitalism as a historical stage in the develo]
of human society bound to give way to another, superior
is itself at fault. That idea has an evolutive and teleolᴜɡᴵᴄᴀᴵ
content, and cannot be denied or accepted except on the plane
of value judgements. It has merely been demonstrated that it
is not possible to provide for the concept an economic foundation within the categories Marx constructed. Capitalist
development takes place with repeated crises and much wast-
age of all kinds of resources. But there has been no persistent
tendency to impoverishment of the masses nor to a decline
in the average rate of profit. The conclusions Marx reached in
his economic analysis are marked by a concern with pointing
out the "serious inner contradictions" in the system. He felt
that the evolution was due to those contradictions, whose
regularities he endeavored to translate into "laws of the movement of society." Thus his entire economic analysis was affected by the method which he carried over from his philosophy. This accounts to a great extent for the difficulty his
followers had in developing the model as an instrument of
economic analysis. Any modification appeared to conflict with
the ultimate objectives, which remained on the philosophical
plane. That is why Marx's model has remained an object of
controversy for almost a century without having been effectively studied and developed. Nevertheless, since it is either
rejected or accepted on the plane of value judgments, it has
become an extremely powerful instrument in ideological
struggles. It has served as the basis of a theory of political
action, opening up the way to the great movements for social
reconstruction that have marked the present century.

THE NEO-CLASSIC APPROACH

Let us now see how the problem of economic development is
viewed in the thinking of the so-called neo-classic economists.
As is well known, in the last quarter of the nineteenth century

and beginning of the twentieth economists put a great deal of effort into circumventing the difficulties that had been created by the theory of labor value. That theory was to become transformed into the most dangerous weapon the socialists had in their rising struggle against capitalism. Marx had founded on it the entire theoretical construction of *Capital*. It was necessary to create a new analytic instrument and to reformulate a whole series of concepts. And the culmination of that effort was the theory of general equilibrium.

The distributivist approach was now to dominate even more powerfully than among the classicists. Cassel, for instance, categorically affirms that the "study of the origin of the existing material goods and forces involved in their creation" has nothing to do with economics, but "lies within the domain of history."[39]

Classical theory never did clearly define what was understood by labor. The distributivistic distortion of that concept led such theory to identify work with salaried labor. The classicists had clearly perceived, however, that in any type of social organization the fruits of the work of a group amount to more than what the members of that group require for purposes of survival. That is why, in any society, there is a tendency to create a surplus social product. Living in an age characterized by rapid replacement of labor by capital, the classics furthermore perceived that the wage-earning class had almost no possibility of appropriating a part of that surplus, which reverted in full to the entrepreneurs and landowners. The neo-classicists, in their concern with inverting the terms of the problem—whose fruits Marx so effectively appropriated —did not take into consideration the existence of any surplus, and sought to demonstrate that each factor receives exactly "its own" part of the product. The wages would not therefore —as the classicists believed—be determined by the supply and

[39] Gustave Cassel, "Traité d'Economie Politique" (Paris, 1929), Vol. I, p. 32.

demand of labor. Implicit in this theory was the idea of a "surplus" of population. The existence of that surplus would in itself be an absurdity, however, inasmuch as the structure of production was determined by the relative availability of factors. If there were surplus population, real wages would decline and the entrepreneurs would be led to apply less capital per unit of labor.[40] Thus, whatever the supply of labor might be, anybody wanting to work would always find employment, providing he accepted a wage in line with the productivity of his work. That wage would be determined by the productivity of the last worker employed.

This construction, so abstract and far removed from the reality of the world of unemployment that existed in the nineteenth century, appeared to the neo-classic economists to be the most irrefutable scientific truth. The uncomfortable idea in the classics that the remuneration to labor was different from that to capital disappeared completely. The latter corresponds to the marginal productivity of the capital factor, whereas the former is linked merely with the marginal productivity of the labor factor. If the population grows faster than the stock of capital, then real wages tend to go down because employment increases at the cost of a reduction in the marginal productivity of labor. But the neo-classic economists—free of the fallacy of Malthus—were not concerned with anything of the kind. On the contrary, their theory gave rise to optimistic expectancies for the wage-earning class: inasmuch as the stock of capital tended to grow more intensively than the population (as was evident), the marginal productivity of labor also tended to grow, and with it real wages.

The great ingenuity of this reasoning justifies our considering it at somewhat greater length. We have seen that real

---

[40] This confusion between long-term and short-term adjustments is a constant in the whole of the thinking of the neoclassics, who made no progress in this respect in relation to the earlier economists.

wages are determined by the marginal productivity of labor; this in turn is determined by the quantity of capital used per unit of labor, by the density of capital. And on what does that density depend? On the relative prices of labor and capital, the price of capital being given by the equilibrium between the supply of savings and the demand for capital. Of course, the same line of reasoning could be followed the other way round, and in that case the element of final adjustment would be the supply and demand of labor. As the neo-classics observe, however, labor does not, strictly speaking, have any "price of supply," for it cannot be used for anything but work. Capital, on the other hand, does have such a price, since besides being used as a source of income it can be consumed.

If the remuneration of capital is given by the supply of savings and the demand for investment funds, it obviously tends to blend into the concept of the interest rate. And, as a matter of fact, the neo-classics did conclude that, in a state of equilibrium, profits would decline to nothing. Obviously, they said, this scheme is a mere instrument for analysis, and the concept of general equilibrium corresponds to an abstract model that helps us understand a reality necessarily far more complex. That abstract model became mixed up with reality in the minds of the economists, however; indeed, to such an extent that the theory of remuneration of capital quite merged with the theory of the interest rate, excluding from the general scheme the concept of profit.

The theory of development which can be deduced from the neo-classic model is simple: Increased productivity of labor (reflected in the increase in real wages) is a consequence of the accumulation of capital which in turn depends on the anticipated rate of remuneration of new capital and the price of supply of savings. Accumulation of capital, causing a rise in real wages, tends to augment the participation of wage earners in the product and therefore to reduce the average rate of profitability of capital. But if the price of demand of capital declines, saving is discouraged and the rate of accumulation of capital drops. We thus get back to the theory of stagnation. As a matter of fact, the notions of profit, accumulation, and development fit into the neo-classic model only as consequences of a shift away from the position of equilibrium. In this position, the remuneration of capital has to be the same in all its applications, and corresponds to the rate of interest. To the extent that the profit or remuneration to capital is in a particular sector higher than average, it is to be deduced that optimum distribution of productive resources has not been achieved, for it is possible to increase the productivity of a factor by shifting it to another sector. As accumulation—that is, net investment—takes place only when profit is anticipated, optimum utilization of resources is incompatible with an economy in a state of growth. Hence, although in the classic model stagnation represented a limit towards which an economy in development tended, in the neo-classic model it is a *sine qua non* for the optimal operation of the economy. This problem, however, was of small concern to the neo-classic economists for the simple reason that they did not pay any major attention to the concept of economic progress.

As we have already indicated, the neo-classicists, especially Marshall, viewed the theory of equilibrium merely as an instrument of analysis. But since it was with the assistance of that instrument that they endeavored to explain the various aspects of the real economic system, the ultimate foundations of their ideas are to be sought in that construction. We have seen that the rate of interest—which establishes the equilibrium between supply of savings and demand for capital—stands at the very apex of the neo-classic model. That rate on the one hand induces the economic system to create savings and on the other regulates the impulses of the investors and submits them to the real possibilities of the system. In other words, there is no point in considering an increase in real wages without first creating conditions which favor the maintenance of a good rate of remuneration to capital. Thus we start out from the principle that wages reflect the productivity of labor and reach the conclusion that the improved welfare of the wage-earning classes is the result of the greater welfare of the capitalist class.

This theory does not bring us any closer than that of the classicists to an understanding of the process of economic development. We know that development presupposes accumulation of capital (as has been known ever since Adam Smith), but this recognition does not bring us any closer to an explanation of the process. Analysis of the factors conditioning accumulation of capital is carried out exclusively from the angle of the supply of savings. Moreover, this same analysis is tied in with an attempt at moral justification of property. This brings up the concepts of *waiting* (Marshall), *sacrifice* (Cassel), etc., which constitute no advance whatsoever in comparison with Senior's concept of *abstinence*. According to the newer approach, the ultimate explanation of economic progress lies in the willingness of a few meritorious citizens to indulge in some form or other of sacrifice. Its starting point is the principle that if there were no remuneration to capital savings would disappear and any accumulation would be impossible. Cassel provides a "conclusive" example in this respect: the hypothesis of an individual with a capital of one million and receiving an annual income of 40,000. If the interest rate were to decline to $\frac{1}{2}$ per cent, rather than undergo so forcible a change in his living standards this millionaire would prefer—in view of his life expectancy—to consume his capital.[41]

All this example does is to show that a sudden reduction in the interest rate, within a specified income-distribution setup, would lead some individuals to reduce their assets. It cannot be deduced therefrom that the community would

[41] Cassel, *op. cit.*, pp. 345-346.

reduce savings, inasmuch as there was no increase in consumption. Cassel perceived, as had Marshall before him, that it is extremely difficult to reduce the causes of saving to purely subjective factors, such as the spirit of sacrifice. But he does not abandon the narrow framework within which the problem had been presented by those concerned with moral justifications. The neo-classicists discuss the problem as if saving depended far more on the moral virtues of the individual than on his actual material possibilities of effecting such savings. To be sure, this had also been the approach of the classicists; but among them this viewpoint is justified, for it was implicit that in talking about saving they had in mind the entrepreneurs alone and assumed that the landowners were utilizing the whole of their income unproductively.

The neo-classicists started with the fallacy that the level of individual savings is determined autonomously, so that consumption is the residual element; according to the conditions of the capital market, the level of savings rises or falls, leading to alterations in the level of consumption. But mere common sense reveals that the basic thing about the individual budget is consumption. It is likewise a matter of common sense that there are limits to consumption capacity, and even more to the capacity for raising consumption levels sharply, especially when those levels are already high. Above particular levels of income, saving becomes almost automatic. This phenomenon became particularly obvious with the advent of the industrial class which—not being an idle class, as were the big landowners—had far more limited real consumption opportunities.

It is interesting to note that Smith had an advance vision of this problem. He observed that concentration of land ownership placed excessive wealth in the hands of some individuals, as at the time of feudalism, who, in order to utilize it—since their riches (income) were mainly perishables—had to redistribute them among a large number of courtiers.[42] It was clear

---

[42] *Ibid.*, p. 384.

that, by determining the distribution of income, the system of ownership conditioned the manner in which it was utilized.

As regards the demand for capital, it was supposed that the latter was elastic in the function of change in the rate of interest. Analysis of this problem did not present any major "theoretical" interest. Now it is well known that the rate of development is mainly conditioned by factors acting in terms of capital demand. Even considering the problem independently of short-term maladjustments, it might be fitting to discuss which factors lead to a continuing demand for capital—that is, a high rate of investment. Indeed, it is a mere matter of observation that during the whole of the nineteenth century the process of accumulation advanced persistently. The average investor always found a place to apply the capital he had available and always achieved remuneration justifying his efforts. The rate of investment had remained consistently high.

It is commonly supposed that the basic difference between neo-classic and classic thinking lies in their respective theories of value, with the "psychological" point of view of the disciples of the theory of marginal utility being offset against the "objective" standpoint of those following the theory of labor value. There is no incompatibility, however, between the thinking of the classicists and a theory of value of the psychological type; hedonistic psychology was common to the thinking of both schools. Suffice it to consider work as a "sacrifice" or "disutility," placing it on the same standing with the concept of abstinence connected with the accumulation of capital, to find a psychological common denominator on which "value" may be founded. The marginalistic theory tended to avoid its psychological content in order to circumvent the numerous difficulties of establishing a precise concept of "marginal utility." The main difference between the two approaches lies in the fact that the mental attitude of the classicists was innovatory—and up to a certain point revolutionary—whereas the neo-classicists held a defensive and to some extent reactionary ideology. The revolutionary attitude of the classicists stands out clearly in their struggle against the residues of feudal institutions. In Adam Smith this attitude appears in the fight against privilege and in favor of freedom of domestic and external trade. In taking a stand against colonialism in his day, Smith sided with industrialization, then nascent in England, against the archaic forms of monopolistic organization of trade. Ricardo, in turn, attacked the vestiges of feudalism both in his theory of distribution, based on the concept of differential rent, and in the theory of comparative costs, which demonstrated how advantageous the policy of free imports of farm products was for England. Ricardo's two basic theories pointed in one direction: towards weakening the position of English farming, which, based on a complex of privileges inherited from feudalism, fettered the forces driving towards the industrialization of the country. It is to this connection with the dynamic, renewing forces of society that the effectiveness of the approach of the classicists is due. Their conclusions may be erroneous regarding the long-term development of capitalism, but they did provide a sound basis for short-term action—that is, for the type of economic policy which was feasible at the time.

Neo-classic thinking reflected right from the start a defensive ideology, the need for circumventing the obstacles created by the socialist disciples of the classicists, and the implicit desire to justify the existing social order as the one permitting the most rational use of available resources. Neo-classic thinking should be qualified as "maximizing" rather than "marginalistic." What is salient to it is the idea that all economic agents tend to "maximize" or "optimize" their positions. The consuming agent tends to optimize his position by maximizing the marginal utilities in every direction; the producing agent tends to optimize his by maximizing the marginal productivity of all factors; and, finally, the community optimizes its product by maximizing the marginal productivity of the various factors. This apologetic attitude inherent to neo-classic thinking comes out to the full in the so-called "economy of welfare," which is still being criticized and liquidated right down to the present.

THE THEORY OF THE ENTREPRENEUR

The interrelationships between the form of organization of production and the accumulative process lay, as we have seen, outside the field of concern of the neo-classic economists. Smith clearly realized the effects that development of urban life had on the form of utilization of the social product. Implicit in his view of this was the idea that the two sides of the process of accumulation—saving and investment—stem from similar causes. Smith's feudal baron, unable to consume the whole of the product coming into his hands, had to transfer it to others for them to consume.[43] If he did not consume it directly or indirectly, he would lose it, for the product was perishable and could not be accumulated. In the industrial economy the problem assumes a different form. Income not consumed can be transformed into productive capacity. This possibility results from diversification of production. Whether the accumulated resources are to serve as a source of future income is an entirely different matter. However, if those resources can become a source of income, as in the capitalistic economy, it is natural that those holding them will ask their price for turning them over.

There are therefore three different aspects of the accumulative process: saving of resources, incorporation of those resources into the productive process (investment), and total or partial appropriation of the increase in productivity resulting from the greater accumulation (the transformation of

---

[43] *Ibid.*

investments into a source of income). What distinguishes accumulation as a process of "capital formation" is the second phase of the process. That is why the theory of development must concentrate on the study of the incentives to investment, albeit without disregarding the other two aspects of accumulation.

It might be expected that the theory of profit, whose purpose was precisely to deal with the problem of incentives to investment, might open up new prospects for the analysis of the process of development. However, the neo-classic economists as a rule limited themselves to "justifying" profit. The theory of "risk" turns back to the value judgements implicit in the ideas of waiting and sacrifice. It is in this respect that Schumpeter represents tremendous progress within neo-classic economics. While working with the instruments of the theory of general equilibrium in formulating a theory of profit formation, he provoked nothing less than an authentic subversion of those instruments.

The basic ideas of Schumpeter's theory had been presented by Wicksell, who, however, was aiming at entirely different objectives. Wicksell used the analytical equipment of the theory of general equilibrium and, as Walras puts it, endeavored to demonstrate that under conditions of free competition profit would tend to vanish.[44] There would remain, besides the "salary" of the entrepreneur, the interest (the element of equilibrium between the supply of savings and the demand for capital) and the remuneration for labor. Wicksell's

---

[44] This concept is fallacious, for the meaning of free competition was never precisely elaborated. In this respect Myrdal—the most critical of all disciples of Wicksell—says that "in reality, free competition neither exists nor has ever existed. It cannot even be clearly conceived, for freedom of contract presupposes rules and regulations about the conditions under which contracts are to be made. These rules and regulations substantially affect the price formation. They cannot be purely abstract rules. They must determine not only to what extent, but in what sense and with what effects competition is free." *Op. cit.*, p. 135.

originality lies not in this observation but in his attempt to account for the general movement of prices through a theory of capital demand which is projected on the macroeconomic plane through the concept of "monetary equilibrium." Wicksell was the first to overthrow "Say's law," breaking down overall demand into consumption and investment expenditure and overall supply into supply of consumer goods and savings and showing that the shifts in the point of equilibrium are due to imbalance between investment and saving and not between the global variables. He realized that the interest rate does not exactly reflect the remuneration of capital, but is basically determined by the banking system, which, with its power to issue script, in practice controls the supply of capital. Underlying the current rate of interest is another real rate, which actually defines the point of equilibrium between the demand for capital and the supply of savings, and which "more or less corresponds to the expected yield on the newly created capital."[45] Wicksell thus shifted the dynamic element to the side of capital demand. His aims were of limited scope, however; he was concerned merely with accounting for the fluctuations in the general level of prices. Since, at a given moment, the real rate is higher than the current rate—that is, if the entrepreneurs suppose that new investment will provide capital with a remuneration higher than its cost—then business will become intensified. There will therefore be competition for production factors and prices will tend to rise.

The basic difference between Schumpeter and Wicksell is one of approach. To account for the fluctuations in the price level Wicksell shows that the driving element of economic activity lies on the side of demand for capital; inasmuch as the supply of capital is a passive factor, the entrepreneurs can take advantage of this to create windfall profit, and hence some pressure on the economic system, with a rise in the level

---

[45] Knut Wicksell, *Lectures on Political Economy* (London, 1950), Vol. II, pp. 190-192.

of prices. Schumpeter did not concern himself with fluctuations in price levels but approached the problem from another angle. It is not that the entrepreneur anticipates profits that interests him, but that the action of that entrepreneur tends to transform the productive process. Hence the driving force of economic progress lies in the creative action of the entrepreneur. This creative action is reflected in the introduction of "innovations" into the production process. Furthermore the action of the entrepreneur is made easier by the existence of the credit system, which makes it possible to obtain from the economic circuit those resources that are necessary for financing the new undertakings.

Viewing the economic process basically from the production angle, Schumpeter found himself in a splendid position to perceive the importance of technological progress as a dynamic factor in the capitalist economy. His approach is therefore entirely different from that of the other neo-classic economists. And it is mainly due to this shift in perspective that his work today appears so timely and is proving so fertile. Even so, he hardly provides a satisfactory explanation of the process of economic development.

One defect in Schumpeter's theory is its spurious universality. The spirit of enterprise is presented as an abstract category, independent of time and of the entire institutional order. It is apparently a gift of the human spirit, as is the "propensity to trade" in Adam Smith. The entrepreneur is presented as a phenomenon common to all social organizations, from the socialistic to the tribal. But we know quite well that the development of an industrial capitalist economy is a phenomenon with characteristics which differentiate it from the development of an economy which is basically commercial or of some other dominant mode.

Though on the one hand it has this false universality, Schumpeter's theory also comes as a complement to the theory of general equilibrium. Marshall's "tendency towards equilibrium" meant the shifting of the system on a single plane. Schumpeter, on the other hand, notes that the system may experience sharp changes, which may lead to a transfer from one plane to another. Thus Schumpeter not only sought to transform the device of general equilibrium into a theory of economic reality but assumed that he had found the key to the formulation of a generally valid theory of profit. Profit would accompany the introduction of innovations but be non-existent in an equilibrium situation.

Actually, Schumpeter's theory is more a theory of profit than an explanation of economic progress. He says, for instance, that he does not consider as a process of development "the mere growth of the economy, as shown by the growth of population and wealth."[46] Elsewhere he asserts: "To produce means to combine materials and forces within our reach. To produce other things, or the same things by a different method, means to combine these materials and forces differently. In so far as the 'new combination' may in time grow out of the old by continuous adjustment in small steps, there is certainly change, possibly growth, but neither a new phenomenon (eluding our theory of equilibrium) nor development in our sense."[47] We are thus faced with a subtle distinction between growth and development. Apparently growth is considered to be gradual whereas development takes place by leaps and bounds.

But it is not only the idea of development that is vague. The concept of "new combinations" or "innovations" is hardly clear. The rise of a monopoly situation he considers as a "new combination." This is not, therefore, a concept necessarily involving the idea of an increase in productivity, reduction in costs,

---

[46] J. A. Schumpeter, *The Theory of Economic Development* (Cambridge, Harvard University Press, 1951), p. 63. See also Schumpeter's *Business Cycles* (New York, 1939), Vol. I, p. 73.

[47] *Ibid.*, pp. 65-66. In the English version Schumpeter eliminated the qualifying "eluding our theory of equilibrium."

technological innovation, etc. It is something broader—"any 'doing things differently' in the realm of economic life"—whose sole constant element appears to be the faculty for creating for an entrepreneur a privileged situation (even momentarily) which would lead to the formation of profit.[48] This idea could take us a long way, because there are thousands of factors creating privileged situations for an entrepreneur and which bear no relationship to development inasmuch as they are almost always accompanied by an opposite situation for some other entrepreneur.

In view of the imprecision with which the basic concepts are defined, one is tempted to conclude that the only practical way of identifying the entrepreneur would be by his creation of profit. Schumpeter himself closes that door to us, however; he recognizes that profit may also be the result of a monopoly situation. While asserting in many places that profit is due to the innovatory action of the entrepreneur, he nevertheless recognizes that there is also the profit of the current monopolist. Although the latter may have acted for some time as an "entrepreneur," he no longer is such. "The carrying out of the monopolistic organization is an entrepreneurial act and its 'product' is expressed in profit. Once it is running smoothly the concern in this case goes on earning a surplus, which henceforth, however, must be imputed to those natural or social forces upon which the monopoly position rests."[49] Thus even as a theory of profit the Schumpeterian formulation is imprecise.

From the point of view of an analysis of development, the greatest weakness of Schumpeter's concept is that he isolates the entrepreneur from the world in which he lives. Why not start from the current observation which holds the entrepreneur up as an organizer of production who—regardless of whether he introduces any innovations—has profit in view?

---

[48] *Ibid.*, p. 86.
[49] *The Theory of Economic Development*, p. 152.

This entrepreneur, whatever the point of departure may be, tends to transform himself into the owner of the capital applied in production and, for a number of easily observable reasons, to benefit from a high income. The idea of a poor entrepreneur helps clarify some concepts but is a long way from reality. What is interesting to observe is that the entrepreneur—contrary to other figures who also have high incomes —is involved in the productive process. The whole of his public and private life is marked by this fact. His energies and his intelligence are oriented towards problems of production. When his income goes up, the entrepreneur reacts first of all as a producer, only afterwards as a consumer. And when his income reaches a certain level, his consumption expenditures become an entirely secondary element, independent of fluctuations beyond that level. At this stage, the entrepreneur's big problem consists of discovering where and how to apply his new income each year. As Schumpeter views it, innovation is not necessarily a fruit of the "spirit of entreprise." It is very often the result of the effort of owners to find applications for resources which accrue to them automatically.

The idea that the entrepreneur plays a separate role is not excluded. Profit—whatever qualifications be ascribed to it— is a residual element. As a rule, then, the most direct means for the entrepreneur to increase that profit lies in reducing costs. This potential provides great stimulus to the introduction of new techniques or new combinations.

Let us consider, furthermore, the problem of increasing returns forthcoming as a result of growth in the scale of production. As a rule, as the business of an industrial enterprise increases—within limits—its unit costs decline. In this we have a typical case of economic growth. No spirit of innovation is called for on the part of the entrepreneur: the increase in productivity is a fortuitous result of the accumulation of capital. Phenomena of this kind apparently lie outside what Schumpeter understands by "development."

The Schumpeterian "innovations" are unquestionably a dynamic element in the process of development. However, the backbone of development lies not in innovation but in capital accumulation. Schumpeter recognizes that innovations demand accumulation of new capital,[50] but he reasons as if the introduction of a new combination causes a leap forward and automatically transforms the productive system. But development is due just as much to the introduction of the new combination as to its propagation, and the latter rides forward on the strength of accumulation of capital.

To accumulate capital implies, in most instances, expanding in one sector or extending to other sectors a superior technique already available. As a general rule, the new techniques presuppose accumulation. Let us consider the simple case of an automatic loom. Schumpeter would view its appearance as an "act of development" creating a margin of profit for an entrepreneur. The next stage, which would have no significance from the point of view of Schumpeterian development, would involve the imitation by other owners of enterprises (not *entrepreneurs*) of the innovation and consequent tendency to a reduction in profit. Everybody realizes (as Ricardo did), however, that the introduction of a new machine into an economy is not an act of innovation pure and simple, for it demands the convergence of particular conditions making it economically justifiable. Indeed, many years after the appearance of the automatic loom manual looms are still being manufactured and enjoy preference in some economies. For the automatic loom to be more economical it is necessary for wages to have reached a given level, and this presupposes that the economy as a whole has made a certain amount of progress in the degree of accumulation of capital.

One can, it is true, conceive of innovations which, without requiring a larger amount of capital per man employed, do lead to an increase in productivity. A typical instance is that

---

[50] *Business Cycles*, Vol. I, p. 93.

of changes introduced into the design of a machine, permitting a greater output of labor per unit of power consumed. These improvements, however, do not arise *ex nihilo*. They presuppose investment in specialized personnel, research laboratories equipped with high cost material, and so on. They entail a social cost not always precisely reflected in the market price, inasmuch as the advance of science and technology is financed by the community as a whole, as in universities and other public institutions.[51]

A theory of development must have as its basis an explanation of the process of accumulation of capital. By isolating the progress of techniques from the accumulative process, Schumpeter created obstacles to grasping the problem as a whole. The theory of innovation is of tremendous importance, but any attempt at formulating it apart from the theory of capital accumulation leads to misconceptions. Nor can the process of accumulation of capital be explained by a purely abstract formulation, for accumulation is closely connected with the system of organization of production, the forms of distribution and utilization of income, and, in short, the entire economic structure.

THE THEORY OF ECONOMIC "MATURITY"

A typical case of special theory in the field of development is that of economic "maturity," presented by, among others, Alvin Hansen. This economist is closely connected with Keynesian thinking, and it may seem surprising that, from an economic theory whose objectives were to explain unemployment (a short-term problem), a theory of development should arise. The explanation is, however, rather simple.

---

[51] We do not exclude the hypothesis—recognized by Adam Smith—that any person who works and has a certain amount of observation and imagination may manage to introduce improvements into the production system and increase productivity without demands for capital.

Keynes, like Wicksell, perceived that the prime mover of economic activity lay on the side of investment and, like Schumpeter, he set about building a theory of investment. But he forthwith realized—and in this lies the fruitfulness of his intellectual position—that as a tool of analysis the theory of general equilibrium was much more a negative than a positive instrument, in the sense that it hampered a reality-bound understanding of the economic process. The best of his intellectual effort thus went into discovering the basic flaw of neo-classic economics.

The working method of the neo-classic economists in the Marshallian tradition consisted of an elaborate application of the principle of supply and demand to the various markets, so as to demonstrate, in each one, how prices were formed and how the trend towards equilibrium worked. Subsequently, the general equilibrium of the system was deduced by a process of analogy. The fallacy of the whole reasoning arose— as Keynes perceived—because in a study of a particular market it was implicitly assumed that the economic universe was infinite.[52] Once one starts an analysis from the point of view of the overall market of the economy—that is, in macro-economic terms, as one would say nowadays—and limits to the economic universe are set, then one finds that supply and demand are merely the two sides of one and the same thing, and that to deal with them as two independent elements in an endeavor to find a point of equilibrium is fruitless fiction.

Leaving aside the notion of spontaneous equilibrium which, according to the neo-classicists, was achieved at a level of full employment, Keynes strives to identify the basic factors which cause this level of employment. Reasoning on a short-term basis and thus ignoring the problems of accumulation of capital, growth in population, technological modifications, etc., Keynes supposed that there are no basic problems from the

---

[52] See Jean-Claude Antoine, *L'Analyse Macro-economique* (Paris, 1953), p. 272.

point of view of supply. The entrepreneurs are acquainted with the cost curves of their organizations and they establish their production schedules in line with their market predictions.[53] The production schedules do not necessarily reflect the productive capacity of the system, but depend basically on what the entrepreneurs suppose the market's absorption capacity to be. At a given level of rewarding prices they surmise that the market cannot absorb more than a particular quantity of each product. This quantity represents the level of effective demand. But the entrepreneurs may be mistaken; the level of effective demand may be different from what they have anticipated. In that case, a maladjustment will appear between real supply and monetary demand, and this will affect the level of prices and modify the expectations of the entrepreneurs, who will endeavor to adjust their production schedules, etc.

Thus the level of production is determined by effective demand. The level of that demand is, in turn, influenced primarily by the oscillations in the volume of investment. The income flowing into the hands of the population becomes transformed into effective demand only if it is consumed or invested. The part which is consumed does not create problems; it is basically determined by the level of income itself. But the part which is not consumed is not necessarily invested; it may merely be saved. And it is here that Keynes finds one of the keys to the problem of unemployment: the disparity between motives which induce saving and those which lead to investment. Whenever within a given economy the impulse to invest is not sufficiently powerful to absorb the whole of the savings formed, unemployment occurs.

In order to expound his theory, Keynes constructed a surprisingly simple model, whose fundamental elements have, however, far more general applicability. In analyzing the

---

53 J. M. Keynes, *The General Theory of Employment, Interest and Money* (London, 1947), pp. 24 *et passim*.

factors influencing the volume of investment, Keynes, apparently wishing to make the system as a whole a neat one, greatly simplified the problem. The level of investment is determined by the anticipated rate of profit (marginal efficiency of capital) and the interest rate. This almost returns to Wicksell's and Schumpeter's starting point. The analysis of the factors inducing the entrepreneur to invest is undoubtedly the weakest part of Keynes' work. However, it is precisely at this point that he apparently abandons the short-term approach and indicates various structural defects of the economic system he is analyzing. A point of departure was thus established for a theory of development.

In utilizing Keynes' analytical tools, Hansen asks: Is the crisis we are now going through (in the 'thirties) strictly a problem of insufficiency of effective demand, or is it a combination of this and a more profound structural problem?[54] Thus he enters into the analysis of development. The nineteenth century, he asserts, was very favorable to development because the farm frontier could move rapidly and the population was growing fast. These two factors, allied to technical progress, provided strong stimuli for investment, leading to the upsurge of an extremely dynamic economy. What we are observing today is a modification in the basic data of the problem of development. The populational curve in industrial countries has reached its turning point. The age pyramid of the population is moving in the direction of greater participation of the older groups; thus there is less demand for homes and greater demand for services, and hence less opportunity for investment. Furthermore, the shift in the frontier and the consequent incorporation of new resources into the economic system are also bygone phenomena. Technical progress continues. In the absence of rapid population growth and a shift in the frontier, the opportunities for application of the current

---

[54] Alvin H. Hansen, *Fiscal Policy and Business Cycles* (New York, W. W. Norton & Co., 1941).

technique based on heavy capital utilization become reduced. The new investments tend to be guided towards growing productivity of capital rather than that of labor.[55] This implies, in the ultimate analysis, lesser investment opportunities. Furthermore, says Hansen, the system has lost a great deal of its flexibility: "The growing power of trade unions and trade associations, the development of monopolistic competition, of rivalry for the market through expensive persuasion and advertising instead of through price competition, are factors which have rightly of late commanded much attention among economists. There is, moreover, the tendency to block the advance of technical progress by the shelving of patents."[56]

We are not concerned with the general validity of Hansen's theory; its limitations are more or less evident. We merely wish to draw attention to its typical features as a special theory of development. To seek to endow that theory with a sense of universality would be a complete mistake; in many countries in the 'thirties the frontier was not yet stabilized, the population was growing fast, and, more important still, the capitalist type of economy had not yet absorbed the whole of the existing population. Hansen's remarks may have scientific value, although they are not universally valid. Their historic dimensions are quite apparent.

---

[55] The investments increasing the productivity of capital in the sense indicated are those which reduce the need for capital. For instance, in improving a transmission system and boosting the power of a locomotive per unit of weight and of fuel consumed, we are increasing the productivity of the capital used in the locomotive. Instead of using three locomotives, we need only two. It is in this sense that the need for capital per unit of product is reduced.

[56] *Ibid.*, p. 363.

2 : *The Mechanism of Development*

A scientific theory assumes the existence of problems whose solution is a matter of concern to some social group. It is therefore essential to recognize the existence of a problem so that its solution may become the object of inquiry by thoughtful men. Economic development, so much the concern of the early classicists engaged in a struggle against the residues of feudalism, has become a "problem" again only almost in our own days. Throughout the period of predominance of the liberal ideology, it was taken for granted that the price mechanism would ensure utilization of the community's productive resources in the most rational way possible. Moreover, the spirit of enterprise, stimulated by the dynamism of a liberal form of society, afforded sound guarantees of economic progress.

Action upon economic processes by central agencies of a strictly nonmonetary type began to be envisaged only when the need for a policy of maintenance of effective demand was recognized. And it was as a byproduct of business cycle theories that ideas about the process of economic development made their appearance.[1] Indeed, although observation of a number of consecutive cycles gave rise to the formulation of "secular" trend theories, it proved extremely difficult to tackle the problem of growth without first understanding the mechanism of such cycles. As clearer insight into the mechanism was achieved, countercyclical policy evolved from elementary measures of a monetary type to coördinated action on the strategic variables of the economic system. Thus one of the most recent forms of countercyclical policy consists of selecting targets to be achieved within a given time by specific sectors of economic activity held to play a strategic role. In a given situation of full employment it may be decided, for example, that to maintain that level of activity—or, more precisely, optimum use of production factors—it is necessary for the social product to increase by X per cent over a given period. Once that objective has been defined and the amount of consumer expenditure—a function of the income level— has been estimated, it becomes possible to indicate the amount of private and public investment required for maintaining the stability of the system. Countercyclical action will, in that case, consist of a series of measures conducive to the achievement of that amount of investment.

A policy of maintenance of a full employment level, while ensuring the full use of productive capacity, requires an investment level corresponding to a high rate of profit. Thus, whenever "planned" investments are carried out without giving rise to major inflationary pressures—something possible only in highly diversified (developed) economies or in periods of rising exports in underdeveloped economies—countercyclical and stabilization policies merge, ultimately, into a development policy.

---

[1] Economic development had previously been the object of attention of historians, social philosophers, and sociologists in the field of social dynamics. See for example the works of Karl Weber, Henri Pirenne, H. Sée, and others, on the origins of capitalism.

In evolving from a price stabilization policy to the coördination and planning of investments, countercyclical action came to need a theoretical formulation going beyond the analysis of causes of fluctuations in the employment level and providing an explanation for the general process of economic development. Hence arose the widespread interest now shown in studies of capital accumulation, of capital-output ratio (relation between amount of net investment and increase in national income), and in renewed efforts to measure national wealth. It explains, moreover, the great significance of *input-output* studies, for they afford a clearer insight into relationships of interdependence throughout the economic system as well as the course taken by studies in economic dynamics.

The point of departure for these theories is to be found in the efforts to make the Keynesian model "dynamic" which were undertaken by Harrod[2] at the end of the 'thirties and resumed with much interest in the postwar period by Domar.[3] These led to the conclusion that conditions of equilibrium could not be accurately defined in the Keynesian model within the limitations of the short-term mechanism it dealt with. Concerned with factors determining the short-term level of income, he had taken as parameters a series of variables such as population, technical level, consumption habits, market structure, capital assets, and so on. Once these elements were known, it became necessary to demonstrate that other variables might be responsible for fluctuations in the level of income. Among these, Keynes pointed to the amount of investment, whose determinants came to be of major concern to him. But, while attributing the role of basic variable to the level of investment, Keynes did not infer therefrom the whole of the necessary consequences. As a matter of fact, he restricted

---

[2] R. F. Harrod, "An Essay in Dynamic Theory," *Economic Journal,* XLIX (1939).

[3] E. R. Domar, "Capital Expansion, Rate of Growth and Employment," *Econometrica,* XIV (1946).

himself to considering investment as an income generating factor. But there are no net investments without accumulation of capital—that is, without increase in productive capacity. Thus capital formation cannot be transformed into a datum of the problem or, to put it another way, into an element foreign to the mechanism for determining the level of income, when the purpose is to define conditions of equilibrium. It is necessary to analyze investment both as an income generating factor and as a productive capacity-generating factor. Once this position is attained it becomes easy to take a step forward and perceive that to reach equilibrium at a level of employment at which there will be net investment, the equilibrium has to be dynamic, to display simultaneous growth of both income level and productive capacity. Conditions for such dynamic equilibrium became the basic concern of those who attempted to elaborate on the Keynesian model. These studies made it possible to improve various conceptual instruments which were to be of much use to economists directly interested in the mechanism of growth.

THE PROCESS OF DEVELOPMENT

The theory of economic development in its broadest form does not deal only with matters of economic analysis pure and simple. This viewpoint is widely accepted nowadays, and it should suffice to cite only the Seminars on Economic Development held by the University of Chicago from 1951 onwards, at which sociologists, anthropologists, and historians have sat side by side with economists. Economic analysis itself can afford an explanation of the dynamics of social change only to a limited extent. Nevertheless it is capable of describing some mechanisms (stable relationships between quantitative variables) of economic development. Some observations on those mechanisms are in order at this point.

Developed and Underdeveloped Countries

The development process involves either new combinations of existing factors at a given technical level or the introduction of technical innovations. For hypothetical simplicity, we may consider as being fully developed at a given moment those regions in which, in conditions of full employment of factors, it is possible to increase productivity (real production per capita) only by introducing technical innovations. This view is not unrealistic, for regions whose productivity is increasing or could be increased by the mere introduction of already known techniques may reasonably be considered as displaying various degrees of underdevelopment. The growth of a developed economy is, then, mainly a matter of accumulating new scientific knowledge and of advancing the technological application of such knowledge. The growth of underdeveloped economies, on the other hand, is a matter of assimilating techniques already extant.

Within the limits of known techniques, there is always underutilization of production factors in an underdeveloped region. Underutilization, however, does not necessarily arise from faulty combination of existing factors. Most often it results from scarcity of capital; and because of that scarcity labor is wasted. Moreover, the average productivity of a mixture of factors in an underdeveloped economy is lower than would be expected from observation of the utilization of those same factors in developed economies. This depressed productivity exists because of the relative rigidity of technical coefficients (no possibility of combining factors except in given proportions) and because technology develops along lines determined by the availability of factors and resources of the countries leading the industrialization process.[4] Thus, if it be taken for granted that underdeveloped countries grow by the

---

[4] The rigidity of technical coefficients particularly affects the sector playing the most dynamic role in growth—industry.

simple assimilation of known techniques (and by the corresponding accumulation of capital), it follows that the transplanting of those techniques almost always implies structural underemployment of factors. This problem can be met only through the adaptation of technology, which is all the more difficult since underdeveloped countries, as a rule, lack a native capital goods industry. In this fundamental maladjustment between factor supply and technological orientation may lie the major problem facing the underdeveloped countries at the present time.

Productivity and Accumulation of Capital

As we have already noted, economic development consists of the introduction of new combinations of production factors which tend to increase labor productivity. Modern technology comprises a body of knowledge whose application makes it possible to introduce new combinations. To the extent that productivity grows—provided there is no intervention of certain factors to be mentioned later—there is an increase in real social income, the amount of goods and services available to the population. The increase in income due to the rise in real product leads to consumer reactions tending to alter the structure of demand. In short, the increase in productivity causes a rise in real income, and the resultant increase in demand leads to changes in the composition of demand and, furthermore, in the structure of production. In the study of economic development it is therefore essential to know how the mechanism of productivity increase operates and how demand reacts to an increase in the level of real income.

We have stated that the increase in the physical productivity of labor is the result mainly of capital accumulation.[5] How-

---

[5] A simple technological innovation may increase the physical productivity of labor. The mere application of depreciation reserves may also lead to increased productivity. The increase in average productivity, however, leads to diversification of demand, and this requires differentiation of supply, which in turn generally leads to net investment.

ever, the relations between those two phenomena—productivity increase and capital accumulation—must be studied in greater detail if we are to understand what difficulties the process of development has to overcome in the initial stages.

When productivity is very low, the satisfaction of elementary needs of the population absorbs a high proportion of the productive capacity. In very backward economies, for example, 80 per cent or more of the active population has to work in order to satisfy the community's subsistence needs. At such a low level of productivity the available surplus for meeting more complex consumption forms or to provide investment is extremely meager, sometimes all but nil. It is therefore extremely difficult for a process of capital accumulation to arise endogenously. In addition, since income is unequally distributed even in communities with the lowest productivity, demand for nonagricultural goods and services by the privileged minorities absorbs productive capacity not employed to meet the subsistence needs of the community as a whole. It might be argued that were it not for the unequal distribution of income there would not also be any surplus for investment or conspicuous consumption. However, what must be stressed is that because of the rapid diversification of consumption caused by a rise in the income available for such purposes income concentration in communities of low productivity does not lead to cumulative processes of growth but rather to static situations of inequality in the standards of consumption of the social groups involved.

Let us take as an example a community of such low productivity that 80 per cent of its productive capacity (labor force) is absorbed in meeting subsistence needs. Let us assume also that in this community a minority of 5 per cent of the population garners 30 per cent of the social product, and that of this half of which is accounted for by foodstuffs and the other half by other forms of consumption. Simple calculation shows that the remaining 95 per cent of the population would have to consume 93 per cent of their income to cover subsistence expenditures. Thus the combination of a low level of productivity with a considerable degree of income concentration implies that almost the whole of the population is excluded from the barter economy.

The main obstacles in the way of development, therefore, are encountered at the lowest levels of productivity. Once the process of growth has been sparked, its own dynamics make sure that part of the increase in income is earmarked for capital formation. But the backward community tends to remain stagnant because it is unable to set the process of development in motion by its own means. Historically, the impulse to overcome those difficulties has always arisen from sources outside the community.

The creation of a flow of foreign trade enables an economy with a low level of productivity to get development under way without previous capital accumulation. As we have already observed, economic development is basically the result of the introduction of more productive combinations of the production factors. These new combinations are typically the expression of technological innovation which usually call for the supply of factors in proportions different from those previously required. Altering the proportions of factors through the introduction of new combinations is carried out through the use of larger amounts of capital per unit of labor or natural resources. Economic development, as currently defined, thus involves increasingly capitalistic processes. However, under specific circumstances, it is possible to introduce new and more productive combinations without prior increase in the supply of capital in complex equipment. This is what occurs in the case of the opening up of a line of foreign trade by external initiative, which allows an underdeveloped economy to make fuller and more rational use of factors most abundantly available to it—namely, land and labor. This is the classic case to which Adam Smith referred when he stated that the division of labor is limited by the size of the market. The increase in real income obtained provides the necessary margin by which the economy initiates the process of capital accumulation. This shows the great importance for underdeveloped countries of expanded world trade. Suffice it to mention the far reaching upheavals forced upon the underdeveloped countries' economies by the persistent contraction of world trade following the Great Depression; some of the countries at the lowest level of development, which had started a growth process under the stimulus of foreign trade, in the subsequent decades lost a part of the increase in productivity they had gained as a result of population growth.

At the outset, the external impulse benefits sectors of the economy directly linked with foreign trade, particularly by creating new profit for the commercial sector. The immediate tendency is towards concentration of the income. There then begins a series of well known reactions whereby capital accumulation and improved techniques first set labor and land free and then absorb them, with a resultant increase in average social productivity. If the impulse from abroad ceases when the average level of productivity is still very low, it is probable that the development process will be interrupted. But once the economy has succeeded in reaching levels of productivity which permit a considerable amount of capital formation corresponding to a degree of differentiation in demand, then the relative importance of external stimuli on the process of growth tends to diminish. As productivity increases, real income grows and demand becomes more diversified, so that new opportunities of investment are opened up.

Growth of Income and Diversification of Demand

As average physical productivity grows through the accumulation of capital and assimilation of new techniques, the community's real income increases. However, although there is a very close positive correlation between those two phenomena, several factors operating in the opposite direction merit attention. One must bear in mind the specific characteristics of a free enterprise economy, in which growth phenomena assume a cyclical form giving rise to periodical unemployment of production factors. Furthermore, the price mechanism may totally or partially annul the effects on income of the increase in physical productivity of labor. Depending on the price elasticity of an export item and the position of the country in the international market, the fruits of the increase in physical productivity of labor in the export sector may, through a decline in prices, be reaped abroad. But, with the exception of special cases such as these, real income closely follows the evolution of the average physical productivity of labor.

Thus the increase in productivity is expressed by a rise in the flow of income. At the outset of a development process impelled by external forces the increase in the flow of income is almost entirely transformed into profit, permitting accumulation of capital for reinvestment, which occurs whenever the constant stimulus of an elastic foreign demand exists. Once the process of growth is consolidated and the demand for labor increases, real wages tend to rise. Additional and diversified consumer demand exerts pressure on prices in various sectors, ensuring that new investment is channeled towards them. Hence the new saving is absorbed in investments supported by foreign demand and in others linked with the domestic market. The new investment also provokes productivity increases in other sectors and the chain of reactions is repeated.

The way demand develops is therefore a basic determinant of the course of new investments. The development of demand by virtue of the growth of national income is, in turn, determined largely by institutional factors. If increases in income are concentrated in the hands of small, closed groups, the process of development started by external pressure will not cause reactions within the economy tending to speed up that process. This phenomenon may be observed in various underdeveloped economies with large labor surpluses where the stimulus from abroad is relatively weak. The benefits from foreign trade accrue to small groups who buy abroad a large part of their consumption goods. Thus the nature of the external sector is highly significant; that is, the type of export economy organized in a previously stationary community. On the other hand, in an economy with large capital assets—a mining economy, for instance—the increase in income is expressed almost entirely in profit; the increase in consumer expenditure benefits a small minority and has limited effect on aggregate demand. The consumption needs of this minority are met by imports, a circumstance preventing the formation of a domestic market and absorption of savings in investments connected with that market. On the other hand, in family-unit agricultural economy, the increase in income occurs almost entirely in the form of wages and remuneration to small landowners. Diversification of demand reaches a maximum in this case. As a counterpart, the rate of saving is reduced, engendering negative effects on growth. Historical experience indicates that the obstacles to economic growth are easier to overcome in the latter case than in the former.

Experience shows that demand tends to become diversified as real wages rise. Surveys among the most varied social groups tend to confirm this tendency to diversity. The demand for food rises sharply in the early stages of development, but the rate decreases once certain levels of real per capita income are reached. The demand for manufactured consumer goods shoots up when the rate of growth of food consumption begins to decline. Durable consumer goods follow a pattern of their own.

Evolution of demand as well as increase in productivity are independent variables in the process of development. With a given increase in productivity, the productive capacity of the economy grows. But unless demand becomes diversified after the basic needs of the population are satisfied, a growing part of that capacity tends to remain idle. At some level of per capita income the only result of development is the provision of more leisure for the whole or part of the population.

New investment is made largely with a view to future demand. As demand becomes more diversified, the structure of the production setup tends to be modified in line with the distribution of increase in real income. It must be stressed that the most widespread diversification of demand is that resulting from the application of income in consumer expenditure and investment. This type of demand differentiation tends to become translated into parallel differentiation in the structure of production as the economy attains higher levels of development. However open an economy may be, there is always a large quantity of goods and services which cannot be imported. This explains why even economies that have evolved towards growing integration into international trade have gradually diversified their productive structures.

THE RATE OF DEVELOPMENT

The intensity of growth of an economy is a function of two relationships: the ratio of investment to income and the ratio of reproducible wealth employed in the productive process to income.

Productivity of Capital

The second of the above ratios may be translated, so to speak, as the average product per unit of capital already invested in the economy. The real capital assets extant in an economy are made up of reproducible and nonreproducible goods. The latter are those found in nature and incorporated into the productive process, such as land, mineral resources, water power potential, and so on. The quantity of these assets, with particular exceptions, cannot be increased by man; their incorporation into the productive process is merely an act of utilization, involving investment only to the extent that it requires labor and application of capital.

The use of new land, for instance, constitutes a real investment to the extent that expenditures are necessary to put it into a state of economic employment. Improvements on the land and farming equipment make up the real reproducible capital in agriculture. The reproducible capital of a mine or a hydroelectric plant are similar.

Considering the economy as a whole, reproducible capital is the sum total of past labor involved in increasing the productivity of current labor. The amount of the product obtained by a community in a given time period thus depends on the quantity of labor carried out during that period plus the quantity of past labor cumulated—that is, the total reproducible capital accumulation. Assuming a constant amount of labor required of each member of the community, the product per working hour tends to grow with accumulation of capital in the productive process. It can be held, then, that economic development is basically a process of capital accumulation.

It would be hard to determine to what extent the accumulation of capital is dependent on technological progress. Undoubtedly without technological progress accumulation would soon attain its limits. But it is no less true that technological progress cannot occur without accumulation of capital, and the former may, therefore, be considered an element of the latter process.

There is no rigid and constant ratio of capital assets and amount of labor to quantity of product per unit of time. That ratio may vary widely, in space or in time. In two regions that have attained the same degree of capital accumulation at a similar level of technique, and whose populations are both working with the same intensity, there may be different levels of production per capita. Disparities can arise from two different causes. One is the degree of intensity of utilization of exhaustible natural resources, such as mineral deposits. There is no necessary economic reason for a region to abstain from intensive utilization of such exhaustible natural reserves.[6] In the course of that utilization it may reach a high level of product per labor unit and unit of invested capital. The second case is that of a relative abundance of inexhaustible natural resources. Some economies are more richly endowed than others with arable land, water power, and so on, or they may have geographical advantages for the establishment of a transportation system.

These observations deserve attention because real per capita income does not necessarily indicate the degree of capital accumulation attained by an economy—that is, the effort already made to develop the region. A particular region may make a great effort towards development and reach a high degree of capital formation per employed individual without its per capita income on that account attaining the level of other regions which have accumulated less capital and still utilize less advanced techniques. Instances of this are seen in Japan and Argentina. The former country has a much higher average capital intensity than the latter, but its per capita income is markedly lower. The abundance of fertile land in Argentina is conducive to a very high average productivity of the capital employed, whereas overpopulation in Japan forces use of less fertile land and inferior natural resources, thereby considerably reducing the average productivity of capital.

Let us now turn from variations in space—that is, from

---

[6] It may be argued that the intensive utilization of exhaustible resources is inadvisable from the economic point of view when it only serves for financing current expenditure. A country or region which does not make investment at least to the extent of the value of exhaustible reserves used will be consuming its own capital. *Mutatis mutandis,* if the fruits of the exploitation of exhaustible reserves are employed to accumulate assets of equal or larger economic value, the policy of intensive utilization of natural reserves will be economically justified.

country to country or from region to region—to variations in time. Within a single country or region the amount of per capita product may vary widely on a short-term basis without any change in the amount of reproducible capital incorporated into the productive process. These variations depend mainly on fluctuations in the degree of utilization of productive capacity. Even outside the cyclical fluctuations inherent in the free enterprise economy, there are a number of factors leading to frictions which prevent full employment of the productive capacity of existing installations. Insufficiency of basic sectors —such as transportation and energy, for example—may lead to a deficiency in the utilization of the productive capacity of many other sectors.

The Coefficient of Investment

The other factor which determines the rate of an economy's growth is the ratio of investment to income, that is, the proportion of current income transformed into new productive capacity. This ratio can be established as a percentage of gross investment to gross product, or of net investment to net product. The second ratio is considered here.

The coefficient of investment reflects the intensity of the effort to grow exerted by an economy over a specified time period. It indicates that part of the product obtained during that period in question which the population does not consume but transforms into productive capacity. In the process of development, the behavior of the coefficient of investment is strongly influenced by institutional and other factors bearing on the propensity to consume.

This problem was hinted at by several sociologists. Max Weber, for example, was concerned with the influence of various forms of the religious spirit (especially puritanism) on the habits of consumers in the initial stages of capitalism. And Veblen—that great critic of neo-classic economics—undeniably displays certain points of affinity with Duesenberry, author of recent important theoretical considerations on this subject.[7]

The Keynesian approach ascribes great importance to the fact that the psychological motivations of the saver are different from those of the investor. But if we switch our attention from the problem of cyclical fluctuations in level of employment to that of growth in productive capacity, we see that it is just as important to distinguish between the psychological motives of the investor and those of the consumer. When a process of development starts in a free enterprise economy the investor is more stronger stimulated than the consumer is. The intensity of growth is closely connected with the initial disparity between stimuli to invest and stimuli to consume.

A specific example will help make this point clear. Let us assume an economy in which the average productivity of capital is 0.5 and in which for some reason or other a process of growth starts—that is, net investment increases to a point where productive capacity grows faster than the working population.[8] In order to preserve the simplicity of the example let us suppose investment absorbs 10 per cent of the net product; thus the coefficient of investment increases to 0.1. When investment rises to that level, the economy in question will start growing at an annual rate of 5 per cent.[9]

---

[7] James S. Duesenberry, *Income, Saving and the Theory of Consumer Behavior* (Cambridge, Harvard University Press, 1949). See in particular Chapter 3, in which he expounds the theory of the "demonstration effect."

[8] In still primitive economies, as noted, the process of development typically starts with the action of external factors such as inflow of capital and technique, foreign demand, substantial improvement in terms of trade, and so on. In countries that have already attained high capital accumulation and whose economies are momentarily stagnant, the process of development may start with internal factors: intensification of population growth, technological innovations, findings of better sources of natural resources, etc.

[9] Assuming productivity of capital is expressed by a coefficient of 0.5

There are good grounds for believing that consumption will not forthwith grow to the same extent as production and that it will therefore be possible for the rate of growth of production to increase. Let us suppose that, in the first few years of development, consumption grows by only 2.5 per cent annually. In that case the growth of the national net product will be speeded up as follows:

	Net national product (a)	Consumption (b)	Investment (c)	Coefficient of investment (c/a)
1st year	100.00	90.00	10.00	0.100
2nd year	105.00	92.25	12.75	0.121
3rd year	111.38	94.56	16.82	0.151
4th year	119.79	96.92	22.87	0.191
5th year	131.23	99.34	31.89	0.243

It can be seen that net investment in this example rises from 10 to 32 over a five year period; the coefficient of investment, 0.1 in the first year, rises to 0.24 in the fifth year. This increase allows the growth rate of the net national product to rise from 5 per cent to 9.6 per cent in the first and fifth years respectively. If consumption had grown at the same rate as net product, the rate of growth of the latter would have remained at the level reached in the first year, as shown beneath:

	Net national product (a)	Consumption (b)	Investment (c)	Coefficient of investment (c/a)
1st year	100.00	90.00	10.00	0.100
2nd year	105.00	94.50	10.50	0.100
3rd year	110.25	99.23	11.02	0.100
4th year	115.76	104.19	11.57	0.100
5th year	121.55	109.40	12.15	0.100

There are a number of reasons why the coefficient of investment in a free enterprise economy cannot spontaneously rise above a particular level. These reasons are connected with the

---

(i.e., that it is necessary to invest 2 in order to obtain 1 at the close of the first productive period), then if such an economy invests 10 per cent of its net national product its annual rate of growth will be 5 per cent.

fact that for a free enterprise economy to grow it has to produce its own market. It would be impossible for such an economy to grow while absorbing the entire increase in national product in the form of larger profits which ought rather to become funds for new investment. Hence opportunities for investment would tend to diminish rapidly and the process of growth would become stagnant.[10]

It is therefore indispensable that a substantial part of the increase in national product be transformed into income available for consumption in the hands of the population. For investment to proceed there must be growth in consumption, and this requirement sets a ceiling on the proportion of the national product that a free enterprise economy can spontaneously invest. Once this ceiling is surpassed the rate of growth of consumption fails to provide incentives for new investment.

In analyzing the mechanism of development we are dealing with a number of models common to modern economies. Nevertheless, the high level of abstraction on which these models may become universal permits only description of some of the general mechanisms of the economic process. At such a level of generalization it is impossible to construct a theory providing a satisfactory explanation of the process of development as we actually observe it. It is not enough to state that growth results from accumulation—including technical progress—and that the coefficient of investment is determined by the rate of investment and average productivity of capital.

---

10 It is in this circumstance that the basic difference between a free enterprise economy and a thoroughly planned economy lies. In the latter, investment may grow for long periods without stagnation of consumption becoming an obstacle. Current investment is connected with a rise of consumption in a more-or-less remote future. Instead of a stimulus to the investor from the market, decisions of central planning organs constitute and enforce development policy. A mechanism of such a type has to be accompanied by a severe adjustment of income available for consumption in line with the amount of goods and services made available to consumers.

It is necessary to get down to the explanation of the concrete factors which determine the division of the national product between consumption and investment. Hence the theory of investment is a fundamental part of the theory of development. Nor are the factors which determine investment to be analyzed in purely abstract terms. At this stage the theory of development has to descend to the historical plane; economies must be classified within a number of pertinent categories. It is in this sense that we refer to developed and underdeveloped economies, to autonomous and dependent economies, etc. The theory of development, instead of being presented in highly general terms, must acquire special formulations relative to various historic processes of development so as to become more precise and pertinent. Thus, in elaborating the theory of development, we may refer to the specific problems of such economies as those of Latin America which have become retarded by comparison with the other economies that developed in the past century and a half. It would be completely unrealistic merely to attribute to today's underdeveloped economies the problems economies now in a higher state of development faced at previous stages of their growth, or even those being faced by economies newly emerging from the colonial system.

The level at which we deal with underdeveloped economies can, then, include only a limited number of useful generalizations. Economies such as those of Chile and Peru present many similarities, but it would be wrong to leave aside some quite dissimilar factors connected with cultural elements in the respective populations, with differences of natural resources, or with the histories of their past development— dissimilarities which impose limitations on the extent to which generalizations on both economies can be meaningful.

A theory must afford means for both understanding and acting upon realities. The proper application of any theory, thus, requires a preliminary identification of problems, and this is not always an easy task. The principle of free exchange, for example, may be admitted as a general rule; but how is one to identify the exact conditions in which this principle holds? How many assumptions do we have to make before we condemn a policy of industrialization of an underdeveloped country on the basis of that abstract principle? Anyone who takes up the study of economic history is repeatedly surprised to see the struggle between common sense and false science. Had the rulers of many countries, including Brazil, followed to the letter the advice of those who were supposed to be well acquainted with economic science, those countries would probably have reached in the long run a far smaller rate of development. A similar observation may be applied even to countries such as the United States and Australia, to select only those where the British economists were read in their native language.

The problem set forth above reflects the clash between the possibility of generalizing and the capacity for explaining. In economics this clash is somewhat more severe than in any other science. The economist, in order not to lose "scientific rigor" and elegance of exposition, takes refuge in a high plane of generalization. When concrete problems arise, he completely abandons substance and retreats into vague shadows. The deficiency can be corrected only by the economist's carrying his knowledge of historical realities much further. A high level of abstraction does not mean accuracy, but rather, that the tools of analysis afford explanation only for a limited number of phenomena taken up in isolation from others. Special cases are left aside, *a priori*. Scientific progress takes place by widening the framework of theoretical constructions so as to make room for more and more special cases. It is undoubtedly quite unscientific to seek to preserve some theory at any cost and transform it into a kind of "Procrustean bed" for problems which exceed its applicability.

3 : *The Historic Process of Development*

From the economic point of view, development consists basically of an increase in the flow of real income—that is, an increase in the quantity of goods and services at the disposal of a given community per time period unit. It is therefore a relational concept involving measurable elements. The problem of qualitative "translation" is supposedly solved by the dynamics of the price system. One item or service is worth more than another strictly because its price is higher during the particular period considered. If that relative price is modified, the importance of the item or service within the computation of the real income is also modified. Such an approach to social realities has been the object of a number of criticisms, even from economists themselves. Quite apart from the cultural factors conditioning demand in every society and, therefore, influencing the determination of prices, there are, for example, relevant problems connected with income distribution and with market imperfections. These problems are of especial importance when we attempt to compare the products of different communities. Let us take a practical example: if the social product of Great Britain is calculated on the basis of relative prices prevailing in the United States, the *per capita* product in Great Britain as of 1950 amounted to 63 per cent of that of the United States. However, if the calculation is made on the basis of relative prices in Great Britain itself, the *per capita* product was only 53 per cent of that of the U.S.A.

But this type of problem is not of direct concern to us here. We shall assume that goods or services which are or may become the object of transactions have a single common denominator—price. Once this starting point is accepted, the economic process acquires the form of a permanent flow of a homogeneous mass—homogeneous because the various components of that mass, although often as varied as a violin lesson or a medicinal concoction, are nevertheless susceptible of aggregation.

The central object of economic analysis consists of a study of the flow of social income. That the flow can be observed and measured from various angles is to be borne in mind in order to avoid semantic problems. It should forthwith be mentioned that income flow is subject to complex fluctuations independent of modifications in the productive capacity of the system, albeit we shall not be directly concerned with this problem here. However, growth of income flow on a long-term basis is practicable only if the productive capacity increases. This, then, is the problem we shall here be discussing: how to identify factors conditioning the increase in productive capacity and the effects of such increase on the behavior of the income flow.

PRODUCTION SURPLUS

The concept of "production surplus" was widely used by the classical writers under the labels *net produce* or *surplus of produce,* meaning the difference between the gross product and the "living requirements of everyone connected with production."[1] In view of the value connotation ascribed by Marx to this expression in drawing from it the concept of a "rate of exploitation," the neo-classic writers discarded it completely. The social product was to be conceived in terms of "costs of factors," savings being viewed no longer as the result of an existing surplus but as the result of an act of restraint or abstinence. From the point of view of the theory of development, in which the accumulation process acquires great importance, there is some convenience in coming back to the classic concept of the surplus, leaving aside as far as possible any intimation of moral values.

It seems self-evident that accumulation basically reflects the productive system's capacity to provide a product greater than what is necessary to maintain the entire population on the level at which the lowest income groups live. To be sure, the fruits of an occasional increase in production might be wholly absorbed by consumption, and there would be a momentary improvement in the living standards of the population without the productive capacity undergoing any alteration. But in every society minority groups have arisen which, in some way or another, have managed to appropriate the permanent or occasional production surplus of the community. This circumstance, extremely simple and universally observed, is the very groundwork of the accumulative process.

In primitive societies the formation of a surplus of production was, as a rule, an occasional phenomenon due to the action of discontinuous and exogenous factors such as exceptional climatic conditions, discovery of better land, external initiation of some line of trade, etc. If the fruit of this increase in production had been distributed uniformly through the entire community, it would have been consumed and its effects would have been ephemeral. Appropriation by a small group made accumulation easier. This phenomenon is even more

---

[1] John Stuart Mill, *Principles of Political Economy* (London, 1895), p. 163.

clearly evident in the more advanced stages of social organization when the accumulated resources may easily be transformed into production factors. And, indeed, the essential aspect of the accumulative process is not so much the retaining of a part of the product by a minority group but the transformation of the surplus into productive capacity.

Accumulation was apparently based at the outset on slavery; that is, it was a matter of total or partial compulsory appropriation by one group of surplus production created by another group. At the most primitive levels of productive technique this seems to have been the most practical way of obliging a social group to reduce consumption to below the level of its production. To the extent productivity increased, it became possible to enforce other methods, for the margin available for cutting down was larger. But the resources appropriated by means of slavery were the starting point for the accumulative process. It is quite true that in most cases those resources were not utilized to increase productive capacity but served merely to raise the consumption standards of the parasitic groups. Even so, they did play a positive role in the process of growth, inasmuch as the raising of consumption levels permitted and often demanded diversification of consumption. The search for diversification became the basis of commercial activities which were responsible for the first revolution within economic processes.

Once a possibility of diversifying consumption through trade had been found, a decisive step had been taken towards the process of increasing productivity. The main lever in the accumulative process, thenceforth, was to be linked not with the restriction of consumption of certain groups by subjugating them to slavery, but with the appropriation of the fruits of increased productivity brought about by the more rational utilization of resources made possible by trade. Once channels of trade had been established, groups and communities arose which were thoroughly dedicated to commercial activity.

Specialization facilitated the concentration of wealth; for a number of reasons easy to perceive, the benefits of increased production tended to become concentrated in the hands of the merchants. And it was this concentrated wealth, in the form of working capital and transportation facilities in the hands of the middlemen, that opened the door to further commercial expansion.

THE SCHEME OF THE DEVELOPMENT PROCESS

With the factors indicated we can now reconstitute the general lines of the development process in pre-industrial communities. In the first place, there are the exogenous factors causing occasional or permanent formation of a production surplus. The permanent surplus, as we have noted, was a result of the system of slavery. Next there is the appropriation of this surplus by minority groups, leading to a rise in their consumption level and consequent need for diversifying consumption. Subsequently the higher standards of consumption of the minority groups afford the possibility of, or even create the need for, bartering with other communities. Thus there is barter trade, which permits geographical specialization and greater division of labor, with a consequent increase in productivity in the communities participating in it. Then comes the concentration of wealth made possible by trade. And finally the possibility arises of incorporating into the production process the resources accumulated by the merchants, this being the means whereby the middlemen can increase the currents of trade and further enlarge their incomes. When surplus production is transformed into a source of income, the accumulative process tends to become self-generating.

This simplified scheme outlines the essentials of the economic development process. On the side of production, there is the formation of a surplus; with regard to distribution, there is the appropriation of the surplus by a minority group; and as for accumulation, the possibility develops of boosting productivity by the incorporation of the surplus into the production process. If we observe the process in terms of timing, we see that the third phase links up with the first. The increased productivity caused by the incorporation of new capital gives rise to the creation of a new surplus which, on being appropriated by the minority group, is also transformed into new capital, and so on. The strategic points in this process are the possibility of boosting productivity and the appropriation by minority groups of the fruits of this increase. These are the two factors which, in the ultimate analysis, make growth possible. If the resources incorporated into the production process did not cause a real increase in productivity, accumulation per se would not lead to growth, merely to postponement of consumption. Furthermore, if the fruits of an incidental or permanent increase in productivity were distributed over the whole of the population, the result would be merely an occasional or permanent rise in the level of consumption and the economy would pass from one stationary position to another without any enduring process of growth developing.

The model we have just described applies to the preliminary phases of development, when both the goods consumed and those accumulated are basically of a similar nature and can therefore be interchanged. That is why appropriation by minority groups is indispensable to avoid consumption absorbing the whole of the product. As production attains a greater degree of complexity, goods suitable for reïncorporation into the productive process tend to become differentiated from current consumption goods. The merchant engaged in the maritime trade, for example, transforms resources he accumulates into ships and other working facilities. The transformations become more and more diversified as time goes by, and the productive setup must achieve increasing degrees of specialization.

In an economy which has attained a higher stage of

development, production develops a structure wherein accumulation becomes an almost automatic process. Hence for the productive setup to operate normally, it is also indispensable for demand to assume particular characteristics. The composition of demand is conditioned, however, by the distribution of income. It may therefore be concluded that the production structure, the allotment of production assigned to accumulation, and the distribution of income all have the same fundamental causes. They are based on the institutional system, which in turn hinges on the appropriation of the surplus.

DEVELOPMENT AS AN EXPANSION OF THE ECONOMIC UNIVERSE

Understanding the process of growth requires having an idea, first of all, of the type of economic universe within which it takes place. Let us, for instance, consider a country such as England in the eighteenth century. Much of her territory was covered by small economic units quite isolated from one another. That territory was occupied by economic units integrated to varying degrees into a national economic system. If we were to draw a map showing these economic units, we should find every possible combination, from the almost completely autonomous community to the community entirely dependent on the other units in the system. Nor would that be all: we should find that the units in which the degree of integration into the national economy was greater were also geared to foreign economies in various degrees of interdependence. We should thus be confronted with an essentially heterogeneous economic universe.

What does this heterogeneity imply, in the ultimate analysis? For one thing it indicates that economic development is a markedly uneven process: it arises at particular points, propagates itself with lesser or greater facility to others, acquires greater vigor in some places, is aborted in others, and so on. It is not and cannot be a uniform process, for each area has its particular cluster of resources and factors.

If the economic universe were to exhibit the same degree of development in every segment, then the application of new resources to the productive process would be possible only by the introduction of technological innovations. Hence we should have for the environment as a whole a situation identical with that of a small isolated community which, owing to diminishing returns in agriculture, cannot absorb further capital without introducing new techniques. However, if the universe consists not of a small community but of a great network of communities, differing from one another in terms of natural resources and degree of accumulation achieved, then the problem of absorption of new capital will turn out otherwise. Whenever an accumulative process starts in one community and there is a decline in the physical productivity of new investments, resources may be transferred to another community in which capital is relatively scarcer. This aspect of the process stands out the more clearly if we bear in mind that the activity which had greatest attraction for new capital at the period in question was trade. The existence of a heterogeneous economic universe signifies, then, that the same goods may be obtained with different degrees of effort in different regions. In these circumstances, transporting goods from one place to another is the fastest and securest way of creating value. Transformed into commercial capital, the resources accumulated in one community, on the one hand flee from the area of diminishing returns and on the other tend to benefit the economic universe as a whole.

If we examine the process in its entirety, we see that the accumulated capital tends mostly to flow into commercial channels which expand and become increasingly inclusive of more and more communities into the overall system. We also find that interchange can intensify the utilization of resources within each community. Thus development in its initial stages is a process of geographical expansion of the economic universe. The appropriation of the surplus by minority groups engenders accumulation and, consequently, higher standards of consumption. In turn, diversification of consumption leads to the acquisition of goods from farther away. The rise of groups and communities specializing in commercial transactions then proceeds to play a role highly stimulating to further development. The considerable appropriation of surplus by these groups makes possible the accumulation of resources required for expanding commercial activities. And the profit motive, which is rapidly spurred by commercial activities, leads to a permanent expansion of the economic universe. Isolated, self-sufficient communities are sought out by peddlers and traders eager for the high profit obtainable in the incipient stages of commerce. Once this commerce is established, there is an increase in the productivity of the community newly integrated into the system, which in turn produces new profits for the groups in control of the lines of trade. Thus additional resources become available for carrying forward greater commercial expansion.

In an economic system of this type, the dynamic element consists of the merchant group, which sets up trading posts, develops transportation, brings isolated settlements into closer contact, disseminates innovations, propagates new methods of production, and so on. Hence the bulk of the benefits resulting from higher productivity concentrate in the hands of the merchants. Enjoying a situation of total or partial exclusivity to purchase or sell, this group manipulates prices in such a manner as to achieve the highest possible profit. The impact on the productive system cannot but be stimulating. The accumulation of resources in the hands of the merchants makes it possible for them to finance opening up new lines of production, settlement of better land, and so on. Productive specialization encourages improvements in working methods. Then these improvements tend to be spread, creating a pool of empirical knowledge which, when introduced into mere primitive communities, again lead to increases in productivity.

Growth in a mercantile economy amounts hinges basically on opening up markets. Once opened, their mere maintenance implies the generation of a permanent flow of profit towards those controlling commerce. Such profits may be utilized in the construction of new shipping, in financing of new enterprises, and so on; thus the economic universe will continue to expand. However, if there is no possibility of opening up new markets, profits will be accumulated in the form of treasure or will be wasted.

Indeed, treasure was not the main form the great masses of wealth accumulated by pre-industrial economies took. They were dissipated in warfare and unproductive projects. Considering the low level of productivity prevailing in the mercantile economies, it is surprising how large a volume of resources was utilized in non-productive tasks. From the pyramids of Egypt and the Great Wall of China to the medieval cathedrals, an amazing number of projects have absorbed substantial quantities of the productive capacity of entire peoples over lengthy periods of time.

APPROPRIATION AND THE SOCIAL ROLE OF THE DOMINANT GROUPS

The form of utilization of surplus production and the social position of the group appropriating it are basic elements of the social process which engenders development. Let us pay closer attention to this problem in its simplest form, examining one community which reduces another to slavery and proceeds to demand of it periodic tribute. That tribute probably accrues to the benefit of the ruling minority of the dominant group. This transfer of income engenders an improvement in standards of consumption and probably a program of investment in unproductive projects or in warfare. With a population surplus available—the slave manpower itself or persons sustained with the fruits of the tribute—construction is undertaken of better dwelling places, monuments, hanging gardens, etc. Alternatively, with part of its own labor force set free, the dominant community may form an army and endeavor to force other communities to pay tribute, thus increasing its income even more. Or it may build defensive walls bolstering its own power.

The ancient empires were formed by this process. Their expansion was limited only by difficulties of transportation and communication and by the military might of other communities. When one community succeeded in enslaving another, the victor became strong enough to try and enslave a third, and so on. Warfare constituted a very direct utilization of surplus production. Development took the form of a temporary agglutination of a cluster of communities. Concentration by a single group of the surplus production of the whole of these communities allowed development of urban life and huge unproductive investments in the dominant community as well as the application of a great number of persons to non-manual pursuits, the formation of intellectual élites, etc.

It is important, however, to note that the dominant summit might be dissociated from the economic tranche of the social process and there might be no connection whatsoever between the pursuits of the ruling élites and basic problems of the economic system. In such cases, the stability of the empires depended on the organizational and managerial ability of those élites. When they succeeded—as did the Romans—in developing an efficient communication technique and a well organized administrative superstructure, their work endured. Once military expansion had ended, a period of commercial development commenced, encouraged by the conditions of security and the improvement in means of transportation which almost always accompanied the establishment of a military infrastructure. Tribute pouring into the central metropolis financed programs of unproductive works. But the tribute could not continue to increase indefinitely, and investment in new unproductive works tended to be limited by maintenance and replacement costs, until finally the whole of the investment resources were absorbed by these costs.

Possibilities of growth through sheer extortion of tribute are obviously limited. However, the political agglutination brought about by military conquest has always had other effects, which are more important from the point of view of development. By bringing into contact communities formerly isolated from one another, by establishing regular means of communication between distant regions, by opening up highways and organizing collective security along them, the political structure was creating conditions highly favorable to the development of commercial activities. With the expansion of these activities, another, more complex means of appropriation of the surplus developed—commercial profit. This change is of fundamental importance, for this profit accrues to a group integrated into the economic process.

It is easy to see that the two systems of appropriation— tribute and commercial profit—have coexisted to some extent all over the world. In the Greek city-state, for instance, we can see both in the urban center itself and in the surrounding rural regions the system of appropriation based on slavery. Side by side with that system existed another one based on commercial profit forthcoming mainly from trade with the colonies. But the latter system was only grafted, so to speak, onto the former; in hardly any case did the two become wholly integrated. Conflict between the respective élites of these two systems of appropriation—with those élites necessarily displaying different ideological perspectives—provided the basis of the great political instability of the Greek cities, especially those in which commercial activities were most highly developed, such as Athens.

The outstanding feature of mercantile economies, by comparison with the tribute economies pure and simple, lies in the system of appropriation by means of trade. The beneficiary class provides a dynamic element in the economic process. In contrast to what occurs in the regime of direct appropriation, the opening up of commercial channels leads to an increase in productivity. The fruits of this increase accrue wholly or in part to the trader. Thus appropriation is more than a phenomenon of mere income transfer; it spurs an increase in productivity and hence the creation of new income. Tribute is a consequence of and enhances the power of the politically dominant, unproductive class or community. The greater the power, the greater the mass of tribute; hence a tribute élite invests surplus in war expeditions. Commercial profit, on the other hand, enhances the prestige and power of the trading class, and the greater the profit the greater the prestige and power—hence the desire to expand trade more and more.

ASYMMETRY OF ECONOMIC REGRESSION

Let us now consider the following problem: What happens to a slavist-and-trading economy, such as those of antiquity, when the political system sustaining it collapses? Most often the destruction of a political order was followed by the institution of a new one; the dominance of one community or people gave way to that of another. This was not always the case, however. The most extraordinary exception to this rule was the collapse of the Roman Empire in the West. The destruction of its huge administrative and military apparatus had far-reaching consequences for the economy of the immense area the empire occupied. The disappearance of urban populations which had sprung up around the administrative and military nuclei deprived the country districts of markets for their surplus production. Under the empire, tribute and trade had fostered intensive utilization of land and of slave or free labor. At that time, as today, it was urban development which led to progress in farming techniques. When the administrative and military system fell apart, the conditions of security making trade possible disappeared; moreover, the loss of tribute brought to an end the main source of income of the urban populations which lived on subsidies or the rendering of services. The towns tended to become depopulated or even disappear. The depopulation of Rome, for instance, was so marked that by the sixth century only the central part of the city was still inhabited.

Here we have a well defined instance of involution of an economic system. Transactions are reduced on every hand, the relative position of production for self consumption increases, productivity declines, and social income atrophies. This example of economic regression illustrates the meaningful and widely observed fact that development is by no means a completely reversible process. Regression does not mean a movement symmetrical with that of progress or growth.

With the disappearance of the Western Roman Empire, there was a process of atrophy within the economy of Western Europe, not a reversion of that economy to its prior status. An atrophied economy stands at a technical level higher than that which would "normally" correspond to its level of income or cluster of natural resources. In other words, the reduction in production per capita, due to the disarticulation of the economic system, does not bring a reversion to the primitive forms of production, does not imply complete abandonment of the more advanced techniques.

An understanding of this phenomenon is of great importance to account for the type of economic and social organization which arose in Europe from the eighth century onwards, the system known as feudalism. According to present-day views, the feudal economy was a closed or nearly closed system. But its main characteristic lay not in that but in its having been a closed economy with a relatively high level of consumption.

The primitive communities of equivalent size—which, like the fief, were also closed or self-contained economies—usually had an average level of consumption lower than that of the European feudal communities. The feudal barons managed with local resources not only to build castles but also to arm their men for war and sustain an almost invariably large number of idle retainers around them. The surplus production which came into the hands of the feudal lord, even if he were of minor importance, was relatively large considering that it was due to direct appropriation of a part of the fruits of the production of a small community. Only the presence of a relatively high level of techniques prevailing within the fief made this considerable surplus possible.

That technical level was, in fact, the residue of an economic system that had disappeared. The feudal economy therefore represented a regressive form of social organization, with techniques in a state of decadence but, even so, on a relatively higher level. This circumstance helps to explain how slavery came to be displaced by serfdom. Slavery reflects the most intensive possible usage of labor. With the advancement of techniques, the pressure against the labor factor is reduced and gradual improvements develop in the systems of organization of work. But during the period we are considering there was not, generally speaking, any technological progress; however, a phenomenon with similar consequences developed, namely, reduction in external demand. When the economy was closed and turned into the fief, available techniques were sufficient to provide consumable production with far less pressure on labor. Consequently, the slave working under rigid discipline measures and iron-bound control on the Roman *latifundium* became transformed by imperceptible degrees into a serf under the rule merely of routine based on tradition.

It might be asked why the average level of productivity was not maintained with intensification of the accumulative process within the fief. The reason is simple: the goods produced could not be accumulated; they consisted of perishables. Without trade, there was no point in increasing agricultural output. The only practicable form of accumulation lay in construction, which attained formidable proportions in the medieval castles. Another phenomenon that might be considered as accumulation was the appearance of large retinues around the feudal lords. If the surplus produced on the fief was not susceptible of accumulation, at least it could find some utilization in feeding a large number of permanent guests. Actually, the number living on subsidies was remarkably large considering the size of the feudal economic environment.

EXOGENOUS FACTORS IN THE DEVELOPMENT OF THE EUROPEAN COMMERCIAL ECONOMY

Taking into account the phenomenon of incubation of a higher technical level, which was what European feudalism amounted to, it is easy to understand how the process of development gathered renewed momentum in Europe from the eleventh century onwards.

For development to occur as an endogenous process in feudal Europe, it would have been necessary for political integration to come about first of all. This would have involved one group's imposing itself progressively on other groups, leading to the formation of larger economic units in which commerce might be able fortuitously to encounter conditions favorable to its development and intensification. Various kinds of factors outside the scope of economic analysis prevented this political integration from occurring, gaining stability or penetrating deeply into the social organism. The linkages formed through personal connections did not have sufficient driving power to permit agglutination of an economic system, inasmuch as they did not require setting up an integrated administrative and security system. As a matter of fact, such linkages reflected the inability of the central authority to govern; they amounted to delegations of that power.

It can readily be understood that in a society of the feudal type any attempt at unification by force faces serious obstacles, for the numerous idle class may choose warfare as its favorite occupation. Any community whose power becomes too threatening to the others provokes their alliance against the threat. Hence any political composition is unstable.

Notwithstanding this, development did commence from the tenth or eleventh century onwards, and advanced rapidly. It was not, however, an endogenous process but was initiated from without. It commenced, as historian Henri Pirenne[2] has perspicaciously remarked, as a consequence of the radical change which the upsurge of Islam brought about in Byzantine trade routes. As a result of the Moslem invasions, Byzantium, the immense commercial metropolis, found itself suddenly cut off from its sources of supply along almost the entire southern and eastern Mediterranean seaboards, and the Byzantines turned with much zeal towards the coasts of Italy. Those contacts, as is well known, propitiated the emergence of powerful mercantile economies along the Italian coast. The propagation in the ensuing centuries of further currents of trade all over the European continent has been extensively studied. Along the European coast a network of commercial entrepôts sprang up and, through the great inland waterways, the whole continent was, as it were, contaminated by the traders' activities. Here we have a typical case of expansion of the economic universe under pressure from streams of trade. Because of the existence of a virtual production surplus resulting, as we have already explained, from the very nature of the European feudal economy, trade took root easily and spread rapidly. The economic universe behaved as if it had been awaiting these

---

[2] See, among Pirenne's works, *La Civilisation occidentale au moyen âge* ("Du XIe au milieu du XVe siècle") (Paris, 1941).

streams of trade, which were to afford better utilization of existing resources and a diversification of consumption without calling for any major changes in the production system.

The currents of trade appeared, then, as an exogenous phenomenon in the feudal world. This is a development of considerable importance, providing as it does the key to clarifying a whole series of problems. It might forthwith be noted that the leaders of the commercial activities were to constitute a new class, the bourgeoisie (literally, the inhabitants of the cities)—a class entirely dissociated from the dominant élites of the surely feudal world. This duality of élites, moved by entirely different interests representing their respective sets of values—one with its power based on land ownership, the other with commercial profit as its raison d'être—was to have a far-reaching influence on the development of European society. In Italy this phenomenon clearly stands out when a comparative study is made of the histories of Florence and Venice.

In the first of the two cities, as Professor Luzatto points out, the two élites never did melt into an integrated whole. The old landlord class upheld its strength and power side by side with the new bourgeois élite, and this duality was not irrelevant to the uproarious political history of Florence. In Venice the mercantile bourgeoisie found the field practically unobstructed and came to dominate exclusively. Venice was unquestionably the most thorough example of a mercantile civilization since the days of the Phoenicians.[3]

Although in cities like Venice and Genoa commerce led to the creation of independent urban economic units, this was not the case elsewhere in Europe. The Italian cities which developed through trade were strictly speaking just entrepôts: they promoted and financed trade between other regions in

---

[3] Gino Luzatto, "Small and Great Merchants in the Italian Cities in the Renaissance," *Enterprise and Secular Change,* in the American Economic Association Series.

order to appropriate a part of the increased productivity made possible by such trade. In Venice, for instance, various rights of citizenship belonged only to merchants called *de extra*—those participating in foreign trade.

In regions in which the bulk of trade was domestic, regions which bartered the products from the surrounding rural area for others from neighboring or distant communities, the unsuitability of the piecemeal political regime characteristic of the feudal world was soon to make itself felt. There then occurred in Europe a phenomenon which was just the opposite of that which had occurred during the shaping of the Roman Empire. In the earlier development, political integration led to trade and development. In the later, on the other hand, it was trade and interdependence between neighboring regions that were conducive to political integration. Feudalism had been the most practical way of maintaining collective security after the collapse of the Roman power. In the stationary feudal world social relationships developed within a clearly circumscribed field which reduced to the minimum the need for government exercising power capable of establishing norms suitable for new situations.

As the currents of trade developed and the nuclei of the new bourgeois society multiplied, the problem of security ceased to be purely local. Furthermore, in a fast-changing society, the field for political action widened, for the coercive and controlling apparatus required continual re-adaptation. Thus the national states arose in Europe not as an agglutination of feudal units but as a sort of "armor" for the protection and regulation of the new urban-based society then coming into existence. This is one datum that should be taken into due consideration in accounting for the speed with which the European mercantile economy developed. In Greece the commercial élites had remained in chronic conflict with the slavist groups wielding political power; in post-medieval Europe the commercial ruling class was able whenever it deemed convenient to ally itself with the royal authority against the feudal power, in short, to take sides in the wars between the feudal lords and precipitate the collapse of the old political order.

TWO SYSTEMS OF PRODUCTION ORGANIZATION IN THE URBAN MERCANTILE ECONOMY

From every point of view the advent of the European industrial economy was a phenomenon whose understanding is of extraordinary importance. In terms of the theory of economic development, this phenomenon assumes highly pervasive significance, for if we come to understand it fully we shall be in a position to get to the heart of the existing economic system, identify the fundamental differences displayed by this system in its various degrees of development, and study its potentiality as a prime mover of economic progress. The transformation of the European commercial economy into a predominantly industrial economy took roughly three centuries of modern history, from the sixteenth to the end of the eighteenth century. For a proper understanding of this slow metamorphosis we have once more to analyze the mercantile economy which developed through a process of "grafting" onto the feudal economy.

We have seen that the European mercantile economy, arising exogenously, did not at the outset cause any structural changes in the feudal economy; the development of commerce as an exogenous process gave rise instead to a new economy separate from that previously existing, even in geographic terms. However, there was no opposition in interests. To the contrary. The basis of the urban economy lay in the potentially elastic production surpluses. These additional surpluses provided the feudal lord with the possibility of diversifying his consumption by utilizing them. Indeed, it was for this reason that the feudal lords welcomed, protected, and granted privileges to the fledgling innovators of the new economy. Thus the development of trade promoted the increase of farming productivity. Some regions of Europe had become specialized to a surprising degree as early as the twelfth century—some in the production of wine, others in wool, yet others in wheat, linen, and so on.

It is of interest to note the typical entrepôt role of the newly thriving cities. Where formerly there had been a self-contained rural economy, there now arose a system in which part of a region's output was earmarked for the foreign market and where from the latter were received, through the urban entrepôt, products which would otherwise not have been accessible. Thus, farming output had to be increased not only in order to provide the surplus needed for payment of the new products from other regions, but also to feed the growing urban population engaged in trade which at that time represented no more than 10 per cent of the total.

A part of the profits obtained by traders from transactions with rural zones was disbursed for products from the rural areas or from abroad, but another (and certainly larger) part of it was spent within the city on goods and services produced right there. Urban production consisted of the manufacture of bread and other foodstuffs, footwear, clothing, ceramics, furniture, and innumerable objects of everyday use. This craftsmanship production was a kind of appendix of the mercantile economy, for which the town operated as an entrepôt. As commercial profit increased and as the expenditures of the merchants within the town rose, there was a growth in the mass of income in the hands of the craftsmen and other groups that earned their living by rendering services to the urban population. It was therefore the great merchants connected with foreign business that, together with their enterprises, made up the central component or driving force of the urban economy. The income of the remaining groups as a whole varied upwards or downwards in line with the level of profit obtained by those traders. Thus the problem of income distribution—that is, the problem of relative prices—tended to be extremely important. Given a certain level of profit to the *de extra* merchants (those with business outside the town), the level of the community's aggregate income might also be estimated. The problem that then arose was to decide how that income should be distributed. Whenever a group succeeded in increasing the prices of its products in relation to the average price level, it managed to increase its participation in the aggregate income.

It should not be supposed that these observations are mere abstract deductions. As early as the twelfth century riots of serious proportions broke out in various towns because of the cornerning of foodstuffs, arbitrary price increases, etc. It was because of these disturbances that retail business operations involved in urban supply early became subject to detailed rules and regulations. It is somewhat paradoxical that in fundamentally mercantile economies the principle already prevailed that intermediaries between the producer and the consumer should be eliminated. Purchasing of foodstuffs from country people outside the urban zone was strictly prohibited. Such goods had to be taken to market and placed on sale at preëstablished hours. No one could purchase more than he actually needed for his own use. These strict regulations were aimed at creating the conditions of a perfect market, that is, an atomized market for both purchasers and sellers. Free competition, if it is not to degenerate rapidly into imperfect forms of marketing, needs—more than any other form of marketing —to be subject to all-embracing regulations and strict control. The laissez-faire regime does not create perfect markets, but provides an opportunity for the stronger to liquidate the weaker or reduce them to a subordinate position. On the other hand, perfect competition, in the form in which it existed in the foodstuff markets of the medieval cities, does not favor the development of a capitalistic economy, for it reduces profits to a minimum. It is in the laissez-faire regime that profit margins grow sufficiently to speed up capital formation.

It is interesting to observe the split in the economic system that prevailed in the medieval towns. On the one hand, we have the laissez-faire regime prevailing in foreign trade; on the other, we have a scheme of strict rules and regulations—either in the form of perfect competition or in that of the guilds—prevailing in the internal activities of the towns. We have brought together the perfect competition and the guilds on purpose, for these two systems in their origins aimed fundamentally at the same objective: to reduce the profit margin to a minimum. It is not difficult to perceive the true foundations of the policy underlying these two systems of organization for production and distribution if we remember that the towns were governed by the great merchants. They had every interest in avoiding rising prices for produce and other consumption goods within the city. With the types of rules and regulations referred to, the ruling classes achieved two objectives: they avoided adulteration or—to use a phrase already coined by that time—unfair business practices, and restricted speculation and large profit margins.

The regime of the guilds, as is well known, was not imposed by the city governments. The guilds arose spontaneously and were made subject to regulations *a posteriori*. The regime actually consisted of a compromise between the craftsmen and the dominant mercantile class. When development of the cities commenced, the number of craftsmen was probably quite small. But as those cities attained a certain degree of development and stabilized, the relative number of craftsmen tended to increase. Nor must it be forgotten that in the thirteenth and fourteenth centuries a bad harvest, a pestilence, or a local war was sufficient to cause substantial disturbances in economic activities. Such calamities subjected many regions to sudden regression. Part of the urban population emigrated, causing a flow of craftsmen to more prosperous centers, often in excessive numbers. Those already located in those towns naturally strove to protect their interests. The resulting organizations were finally made subject to regulations enforcing two objectives: those of tradesmen seeking to protect themselves against the intruders, and those of the ruling class attempting to maintain the quality of production while holding down local prices. The craftsmen had to be satisfied with moderate profits but in compensation were granted market exclusivity.

The compromises which underlay the guild system can be distinguished more clearly in the light of what has been said about the importance of the problem of income distribution in the economy of the towns. The overall level of income, determined by the amount of profit which chance provided the great merchant class, was the independent variable. If the merchants reduced their expenditures, the artisans' incomes dropped and they in turn reduce their expenditures, leading to further reductions in income. The shrinkage in the merchants' expenditures thus over a given period of time led to overall reduction in income, the size of this reduction depending upon the multiplier factor. But let us return to the central factor. Given a specific level of aggregate income, that income had to be distributed among the various groups of the community. The relative prices—that is, the domestic terms of trade—were therefore the big issue in these communities. If we observe the medieval economy from this angle, we see that the guild system embodied not only a compromise between each artisan group and the governing class, but also a compromise among the various craftsman groups themselves. The status quo of income distribution was accepted; no one had the right to complain. Each class, in turn, undertook to divide up between its members the quota to which it was entitled.

The internal operation of a typical medieval urban economy, viewed in the light of the factors we have described, shows several similarities with that of the feudal economy. It is quite true that an urban economy forms a part of the current of trade, whereas the fief is mainly a self-contained economy. But from the point of view of their internal operations these two types of economies present fundamental likenesses. In the fief the income is distributed on the basis of the level of the harvest—which in this case is the independent variable—in line with an established tradition. That tradition tends to benefit the land-holding group. In the town, once the level of aggregate income is set, distribution likewise takes place in conformity with a series of strict norms, albeit now tending to benefit the ruling mercantile group and effecting compromise among the artisan groups. In both cases there is a system of organization for production entirely lacking a growth impulse of its own. In fact, from this point of view the medieval urban economy is much more similar to the feudal economy than to the industrial economy. However, the medieval urban economy also differs from the feudal economy in one significant way: it has a dynamic factor—the large mercantile class. That class grew up, as we have pointed out, as an intermediary for trade among regions producing primary goods and between them and regions producing more elaborate articles. With the development of urban life and the diversification of consumption among the governing groups in the rural regions, various manufactured products (especially high quality textiles) came into growing demand. At the outset the textile trade was limited to high-priced products imported mainly from the East. With the increase in consumption, the merchants soon perceived the advantage of providing direct incentives to the production of such textiles. By the twelfth century the production of textiles for export was being carried out on a considerable scale in a number of towns and was controlled by merchants who financed it and supplied the raw materials. This type of urban production for export appeared earliest in Italy and in the thirteenth century gained considerable impulse in Northern France and the Netherlands. Textiles of these origins began to be exported on a large scale, even to the East, through the Genoese merchants.

Urban manufacture for export was entirely different from that of guild craftsmanship. The reasons for the difference are fairly simple. Guild craftsmanship was organized in order to meet a regular, relatively stable demand, but manufacture for export depended on a number of hazardous factors connected with the foreign market. In the foreign market competition of the laissez-faire type predominated. The quantities placed on that market might be large or small, depending upon conditions prevailing at the particular period of time. Loss of a ship, due to piratry or storms at sea, might entail total loss for one merchant and perhaps extraordinary profits to a number of others. Thus faced an extremely curious situation persisted throughout the Middle Ages and until the beginning of modern times: Within the urban communities production tended to become organized so that all unforeseen circumstances were eliminated; but among those same urban communities business was carried on under entirely unpredictable or highly venturesome conditions. It was the second type of trade that, with its dynamic impulse and instability, was to bring about successive and increasingly far-reaching breaches in the general framework of the system.

TENSION ON THE LINES OF TRADE; THE GROWING IMPORTANCE OF THE PROBLEM OF COSTS

From the fourteenth century on, the great lines of trade began to display symptoms of saturation. The commercial frontier had pushed to the farthest boundaries of Europe and the economic environment had to draw back under pressure from the Ottoman invasions. Competition intensified and tension within the system increased. The situation was to favor the political unification of the European national states. Just as the craftsmen had organized so as to defend themselves within the city limits, so also the great bourgeoisie, which favored political unification, was to organize for self-defense within the national frontiers. In England during the first half of the fourteenth century the royal government endeavored to prohibit the import of textiles. In that same century, the same government also strove to reserve trade along the country's coastal waters to English vessels exclusively. England, later to become the first country to engage in a markedly free-trade policy, was thus the first country in Europe to formulate and apply a decidedly protectionistic policy. The English protectionistic policy caused vigorous reactions, especially in the Netherlands, where imports of English textiles were prohibited.

The growing tension in European trade, brought about by increasing competition, could not but have repercussions on the system of production organization. Costs began to be of increasing significance. It was necessary to reduce costs in order to counterbalance customs tariffs. In order to compete with protected local enterprises becoming more and more organized, it was necessary to reduce costs even further. Thus a gradual shift occurred from an economic system in which the margin of profit was extremely high or loss was total to one with greater security in transactions and greater regularity in operations but smaller profit margins.

The relative importance of cost of production in the composition of the profits depends on the type of commercial operation involved. In the primitive type of trade, the relation between cost of production and sale price for a given line of merchandise was somewhat remote. Let us consider, for instance, the case of a product such as sugar. Small quantities came from the East to be sold in Western Europe. The cost of production of sugar, or, rather, the price paid to the producer probably did not amount to as much as 5 per cent of the sale price to the ultimate consumer. That price went almost entirely to the middleman (who ran the risks of transporting the product through unsafe regions during a period of months), to cover tolls and dues, and to provide a profit to the merchant. The cost of production thus bore no relationship to the sale price. What interested the merchant was safety in transportation, for the loss of a cargo represented a tremendous setback. Hence the investments made in outfitting ships, protecting caravans with armed groups, and so on. Such investments were enormously more rewarding than any possible reduction in costs of production could be.

The terms of this problem began to change with the intensification of competition in Europe. For the Flemish merchant financing the production of woolens for export to England, production costs began to be a factor of importance. The businessman imported the wool and the dyes and contracted for production of the goods with a master weaver. The master, in turn, farmed out the job to others, who worked in their own homes. With intensification of competition, the financing merchant began to concern himself with costs, so as to be able to stay in business. The master weaver, who in this case acted as a production manager, then strove in every possible manner to reduce his costs; the alternative was to lose the job. As a result, collective producing organizations—"factories"— began to arise, whose objective was to intensify the use of the working tools and facilitate the control of raw materials, number of working hours, etc. An effort was also made to use women or child workers as much as possible, also with a view to cutting down on costs. These transformations in the form of production organization aroused terrific resistance in some quarters. Three centuries of adjustment and readjustment, pressure and distortion, had to elapse for a complete metamorphosis to come about. The greatest resistance arose in the sector of the guilds, which had enjoyed a set of privileges and strove in every way possible to prevent production within city areas on a basis of "free labor"—as it was then called—organized by master traders. These, on the other hand, endeavored to organize production in rural areas, or went to towns in which guilds had not yet been organized, or found other means of getting around the difficulties.

The important thing to consider in all this is that a new system of organizing production had arisen in which costs played a fundamental role. One of the first consequences of the consolidation of this system was the pressure against the real wages of the craftsmen who had become laborers. At a primitive level of techniques the main component of operational costs was the payroll. It was necessary to reduce that payroll and every possible method was used to that end. Working conditions in the second half of the eighteenth century—when the final overthrow of the guilds took place—and at the beginning of the nineteenth century were in no way better than they had been under the Roman Empire. Pressure against the labor force reached a peak and, without any alteration having occurred in the juridical relationships prevailing in society, the working regime acquired characteristics of duress such as had not been known in Europe for the entire preceding thousand years. Yet reducing payroll is only one of the ways of holding down production costs. The entrepreneurs early realized that the needs of subsistence limit that method. But they also soon perceived that by modifying production methods, making a better division of labor, and introducing more adequate working tools they could go far further than by merely cutting down on wages. Apparently the increases in productivity which had already been achieved in the eighteenth century with a more rational division of labor had been stupendous. Indeed, Adam Smith, when he published his *Wealth of Nations* in 1776, ascribed all increases in productivity to improvements in the division of labor.

There is no point in going into details regarding the complex and far-reaching transformations the European economic system underwent from the eighteenth century onwards. We should, however, draw attention to one phenomenon of considerable importance—the progressive enhancement in techniques of production to the point where they became the very crux of the economic system. The outstanding steps of the process began with contraction of the economic frontier in Europe spurring intensified competition. Consequent growing tensions speeded up the agglutination of the political system, building up national economies, and the rise of the mercantilist policy of protection of the national bourgeoisies. In order to maintain their lines of trade, especially those for textile exports to neighboring regions, the merchants demanded that the master craftsmen (the production managers) obtain lower and lower costs. As a result, a class of craftsmen-entrepreneurs arose whose living depended on permanent tightening of production costs. The policy of cost reduction led to the organization of great producing centers—the factories—and tremendous pressure against real wages; as a corollary of this policy of reduction of costs, progressive improvements occurred in production techniques. Thus a succession of extraordinary possibilities began to unfold.

PRODUCTION TECHNIQUES AS A FOCAL POINT OF THE NEW ECONOMIC SYSTEM

We shall not diverge to consider the manifold aspects of this fascinating problem of the emergence of an industrial economy, but shall merely note a few points of special interest from the angle of understanding the highly dynamic nature of this economy. The first point concerns the tremendous value attached to empirical research. Since industrial production is merely a means of transforming and adapting natural resources through processes based on principles derived from observation of the physical world, the desire to improve production techniques called for increased knowledge of the natural resources and of the physical world in general. To be sure, a desire to understand and explain the physical and metaphysical world has been common to all cultures. It was only in the industrial economy, however, that this fundamental impulse of the human mind became incorporated into the driving element of the economic system. It is easy to understand the explosive force that was to result from the conjunction of these two basic impulses of mankind: the desire for wealth and power and the yearning for understanding and interpreting the world we live in. In contrast, these two factors completely failed to unite in the Greek world because the commercial élite remained as it were grafted onto the social organism while the ideological framework of the landlord-slavist élite continued to prevail. Yet in itself the predominance of the commercial élite would not have been sufficient to achieve that extraordinary combination which crystallized only in the eighteenth century; the typical development of commercial economies was to follow the line of least resistance afforded by continual displacement of the economic frontier. The Phoenicians, for example, reached England and the Portuguese went as far as India. Hence the economic densities of their respective environments remained too meager for the organization of production to become a matter of concern.

The second point to which we would draw attention concerns the new investment opportunities which arose with the industrial economy. Improvement in production methods obviously presupposes concomitant progress in knowledge of the physical world and consequently ascribes greater value to the natural sciences. But that is not all. It also requires incorporating additional resources into the productive process. The methods of production were to become—in the nineteenth century terminology—increasingly capitalistic, based more and more on the use of equipment and other forms of capital. This was to have far-reaching consequences on the organization of the economic system, for in order to invest reproductively resources which are constantly flowing into his hands the entrepreneur no longer needs a frontier for expansion. He no longer seeks to open up new lines of trade, but can apply his capital in depth, so to speak, within the already established economic universe. The application of capital fosters increased productivity, rise in aggregate income, and therefore expansion of the domestic market. By reducing costs without cutting down on wages, the entrepreneur can reduce the prices of his products while leaving the income of his workers intact. Hence the profit coming into the hands of the industrial entrepreneurial class is applied within the industrial system itself.

The essential framework of the economic system which grew to maturity in the nineteenth century involved, then, the industrial entrepreneur who placed his products in a market in which the prices are formed independently of his will; sales prices of the final products were—for the individual entrepreneur—a mere datum on the basis of which he endeavored to organize production. On the other hand, that same entrepreneur organized his production on the basis of factors and resources that he acquired in the various markets at price levels also beyond his control. It is between these two markets —the final product market and the production factor market— that the industrial entrepreneur operated. His main concern lay in taking the utmost advantage of the factors he acquired —in other words, in organizing production as efficiently as possible. Hence the key to this economic system lay in organization and production techniques. Nor is that all: introducing innovations in production techniques usually opened up opportunities for capital—flowing into the entrepreneur's hands in the form of profit—to be reincorporated into the production system. Productive efficiency and the advancement of techniques thus achieved for the new economic system both a source of profit for the entrepreneur and an opportunity of applying that profit remuneratively. Thus technology came to play the role of a central dynamic factor in the industrial economy. And as technology is nothing more than the application to the productive system of scientific knowledge about the physical world, it may be stated that the industrial economy is limited only in the ability of man to acquire knowledge of the world he lives in.

GROWTH AND INSTABILITY AS INHERENT FACTORS OF THE FREE ENTERPRISE INDUSTRIAL ECONOMY

We have noted in the preceding sections that production costs are the basic problem of an industrial economy. We have also observed that concern with costs was responsible for bringing production techniques into the foreground and that the process of development therefore tended to become a process of technological progress. Finally, we indicated that progress in technology provided opportunities for constantly accumulating capital to become incorporated into the productive process. Given these circumstances, the industrial economy, unlike the commercial economies, does not require an expanding geographical frontier in order to be able to grow. Its development takes place basically in depth. Furthermore, growth is an inherent aspect of the system of the industrial economy and not a mere contingent as in the case of the commercial economy. One cannot conceive of an industrial economy except in terms of growth, for the fundamental parts of its setup acquire definite form and become individualized only through growth. A theory of industrial economy must necessarily include an explanation for economic growth.

Let us view the problem more closely. In the mercantile economy the level of income is determined, as we have seen, by the profits of the great commercial class. Let us consider the example of the Genoese merchants who purchased textiles in North France and the Netherlands for sale in the ports of the Levant. The profits collected by those merchants were spent largely within the city of Genoa, flowing into the hands of craftsmen and local suppliers of services, who indulged in other expenditures in the city markets, including the purchase of foodstuffs from the surrounding rural areas. However, the great merchants did not consume the whole of their profits. As we have already noted, the way in which income is distributed in a commercial economy prevents that income from being entirely consumed. Only a part of the great mass of income flowing into the hands of the merchant is used for current consumption expenditures. The remainder has to be reinvested. The merchant may expand his business, have ships built, purchase larger quantities of raw materials for supplying the artisans, and so forth. It is possible, however, that the flow of trade may become saturated, that with increasing competition our merchant cannot reïnvest his profits productively. In that case he may apply them in nonproductive investments: luxury mansions, objects of adornment, donations to religious organizations, dowries for his daughters, and so on. In the last resort the merchant may store up his wealth as pure monetary treasure. It must be realized that the merchant's profit in the case in question is a monetary one. Once the operations of buying and selling have been carried out, the remainder that stays in his hands takes the form of precious metals, which may be accumulated and left indefinitely in reserve. It was on that account that the great mercantile cities soon turned into centers of credit, and many commercial houses came to operate as banking houses. But what we want to emphasize here is that, quite independent of the application which the merchant chooses for the increment of the mass of income coming into his possession, the economic system continues to operate normally. That fact is of great importance if one is to understand the way mercantile economies operate. They develop rapidly in their initial stages, but once they have reached a maximum point of development they become stationary and remain at that point until some exogenous factor jolts the balance.

If we proceed from this picture of the commercial economy to consideration of the mechanism of the industrial economy, we perceive forthwith the sharp distinction between the two systems. In the industrial economy profit retains its fundamental characteristics of being a residue. Once the services of the various production factors have been paid for, the entrepreneur endeavors to sell his product at the highest possible price. Depending upon that sale price, the profit—which is residual—is larger or smaller. But the important thing to bear in mind here is that the profit has been incorporated into the price of the product. Taking an industrial economy as a whole, we find that within the value of each article sold are included the payments for all factors participating in its production. The price of a yard of cloth is basically the sum of the payments for labor (wages), capital (interest, rental, lease of land, etc.), and the entrepreneur (profit). In paying for labor and other factors in advance of sale, the entrepreneur carries out a credit operation; he is advancing a part of the value of a yard of cloth that is going to be sold in the future. On the other hand, when he sells his yard of cloth the entrepreneur gets back not only those payments he has already made but also an additional payment which constitutes the profit. Hence this additional payment amounts to a kind of credit operation in reverse: it is an amount of income incorporated into the value of the yard of cloth sold, and which remains in liquid form in the hands of the entrepreneur. In other words, the profit coming into the possession of the entrepreneur is the counterpart of the value of other goods which are being produced and have not yet been sold. Thus if the aggregate value of all goods sold over a given production period is equal to the sum of payments to overall production factors, and if the entrepreneur sells a good and withholds in liquid form a part of its value, then obviously that withholding makes it impossible for other goods to be sold.

If we regard the process of formation and utilization of income from this angle, we observe the sharp difference between industrial and mercantile economies. In the latter, the income of the great merchants could be kept partly in a liquid form and treasured up indefinitely. Being gleaned outside the economic system of the urban community, that income had no counterpart of goods in production within that system. In the industrial economy the income of the entrepreneur, just like that of the wage earner or that of anyone else, must be fed back into the economic circuit. If one entrepreneur retains his profits as liquid assets,[4] then another entrepreneur will not be able to sell the totality of his production. That is why, in the industrial system, production is organized in advance in line with expectations of how income will be utilized, with due account being taken of the possibilities of external trade. To operate without difficulty, the system not only requires that total income be used but also that it be utilized more or less in a specific manner. Hence the great instability of industrial economies.

But to return to the main point at issue. We have seen that the basic characteristic of the industrial economy is that within it the entrepreneur endeavors to reïnvest his profits by perfecting his production methods. However, bearing in mind the remarks made above, we shall see that no less a specific feature of the industrial system is the fact that the entrepreneur cannot refrain from reïnvesting his profits, that is, that part of his income that he fails to consume. The industrial entrepreneur, like the character in a famous medieval legend, has a "demonic hand" which equips him to solve all his problems. But woe betide him if he fails to make that hand accepted by another person, if he fails to reïntroduce into the economic circuit the profit that comes into his possession. If he retains that profit in liquid form he leaves a part of the output of other entrepreneurs without a buyer. They in turn will take

---

[4] The banking system developed in order to serve as an intermediary between persons accumulating liquid assets and those with an enterprising disposition and wishing to invest. The remark pertains, therefore, to an economy as a whole.

steps to defend themselves by reducing their own volume of business, thus reducing the income of other groups. More merchandise will be left without buyers, and the ruin of a large number of entrepreneurs ensues. Thus, unlike the mercantile economies, which could remain in a stable situation for centuries, the industrial economy is fated to grow or else decrease.

In a free enterprise economy, in which a particular type of income distribution necessarily prevails, a great mass of income is constantly formed which does not get used for consumption. This income, as we have seen, cannot be taken out of the economic circuit without causing far-reaching disturbances. The big issue is therefore how to invest it. This requires adequate development of those lines of production demanded by the process of investment.[5] The structure of the productive system therefore reflects the form of utilization of the income and this in turn, within a free enterprise economy, is determined by the manner in which that same income is distributed. Hence problems of development must be considered simultaneously as problems of production and distribution.

If we view the industrial free enterprise economy from this angle we see that in order to utilize productive capacity to the full it must continually transform into capital a great mass of income. In other words, to be able to operate normally, the system must increase its productive capacity continually. This feature of the system is the basis for contending that growth is an inherent factor of this type of economy. Moreover, this organic need for growth contains the seed of the great instability of the free enterprise industrial economy. Entrepre-

---

[5] Foreign trade affords more elasticity to the structure of supply, facilitating adjustments between supply and demand through the process of growth. The reasoning presented may be rigorously applied if we consider the whole of the national economies or a single self-contained economy.

neurs have at their disposal quite imprecise means of guidance in drawing up their investment plans; hence they usually invest too much in one sector and too little in another. The capital markets have developed in order to get around difficulties of this kind, permitting broader recruitment of the entrepreneurial class and providing more systematic information regarding business prospects. For a free enterprise industrial economy to develop without "ups and downs" it would be necessary for the entrepreneurs to be able to foresee the precise future behavior of consumers and to arrange collectively not to overinvest in some sectors and underinvest in others. Nor is that all. It would also be necessary for the capital goods industries to know precisely the equipment needed for production growth within the scheme established among the entrepreneurs.

These remarks should suffice to show that by its very nature a free enterprise industrial economy cannot develop in linear fashion. A succession of alternating phases of great accumulation of capital and phases of depression is "normal" to the growth of such an economy. This broad pulsation of the economic system, which economists for the past century have been calling the business cycle, is the counter coin of the process of growth of the free enterprise industrial economy.

4 : *Elements of a Theory of Underdevelopment*

THE CLASSIC MODEL OF INDUSTRIAL DEVELOPMENT

The theory of development, as conceived in the great university centers of the Western world, has the limited purpose of revealing the nature of those extra-economic variables which in the ultimate analysis are responsible for the rate of growth of production in an economy.[1] In a given economic structure the fundamental processes involved must be traced so as to permit identification of the exogenous variables which cause instability in the rate of growth and determine its intensity. The numerous models of development appearing in the current bibliography carry through from this line of thought. This perspective, however, presents a fundamental flaw in ignoring

---

[1] Nicholas Kaldor, "A Model of Economic Growth," *The Economic Journal*, December, 1957. Identical presentations of the theory of economic growth are to be found in Harrod, "An Essay in Dynamic Theory," *Economic Journal*, March, 1939, and *Towards a Dynamic Economics* (Macmillan, 1948), as well as Domar, "Capital Expansion, Rate of Growth and Employment," *Econometrica*, April, 1946, and "Expansion and Employment," *American Economic Review*, March, 1947. Much of the extensive literature on the theory of economic growth published during the past ten years is mere refinement of the basic model presented by Harrod and Domar.

the intrinsic historic dimension of economic development. A theory of development which merely reconstitutes in an abstract model—derived from a limited historic experience— the articulations of a given structure cannot presume to attain a high degree of generality. Furthermore, the problem is not restricted to the level of development achieved by the various economic systems coëxisting at a given moment of history. It must be borne in mind that the economic development of the past two centuries—the Industrial Revolution, as it is currently labeled—is itself a unique historic phenomenon. Actually, the advent of an industrial economy in Europe during the last few decades of the eighteenth century, entailing a disruption of the world economy of the time, involved a qualitative change of the same order as the discovery of fire, of the wheel, or of the experimental method.

Prior to the Industrial Revolution, economic development was mainly a process of agglutination of small economic units and of geographical division of labor. The dynamic agency of development consisted of the commercial class. By promoting the agglutination of economic units into larger markets, it created more complex forms of division of labor and made possible geographical specialization. The fruits of the resultant increase in productivity were largely absorbed by the ruling groups presiding over the communities engaged in promoting trade, and this made substantial concentrations of financial capital possible. However, since there was little or no articulation between the commercial and the productive groups, accumulation of profit in the hands of traders had little or no effect on production techniques. From the point of view of the traders of those days, the most lucrative investment lay in opening up new labor fronts or financing the destruction of competitors. Only in very special cases were they concerned with production methods.

We have seen in previous chapters the factors which led to the advent of an industrial type economy in eighteenth century Europe. Once this first industrial nucleus had taken shape, factors conditioning the behavior of the world economy underwent rapid and radical transformation. Essentially these transformations concentrated at two points. The first involved the causal factors giving rise to growth, which became endogenous to the economic system. The second, a particular aspect of the first, involved the imperative need for technological progress and its dependence on a close connection between the capital formation process and the advance of experimental science.

In pre-industrial economies, profits when due to operations within the economic system itself and not to external trade, largely consisted of direct appropriation of goods and services at the disposal of the community. The profit of the farm proprietor, for example, consisted of that portion of the product from the land which was left in his hands for the sustenance of his family and other dependents. The trader's was derived from goods and services directly consumed, as well as from the gold he was able to treasure up, and which permitted him to increase his business turnover. If stockpiles at the end of the year were greater than desired, he planned to reduce purchases, and everything returned to normal. This easy type of adjustment cannot occur, however, in an industrial economy. Industrial profit, being a payment to a production factor (the activity of the organizer or entrepreneur), is necessarily incorporated into the sale price of the article at the moment when the latter passes from the producer's hands into those of the trader. Jointly with payments to other factors, it is the financial representation of a production operation. Hence it acquires social value only when the good produced is sold to the ultimate consumer. Until that time, any payment to production factors is a mere credit operation. If all production is to be bought, the aggregate sum of payments to factors during production must be expended. If the producer cannot find a buyer and his goods stock tend to pile up, then the industrial entrepreneur, unlike the trader, will not be in a position to transfer the pressure to an endless series of craftsmen or domestic producers. If he wants to liquidate the stockpiles involuntarily accumulated and still remain in business, he has to put the merchandise up for sale at a lower price. That is why production costs are a matter of primary concern to him.

From the point of view of the industrial entrepreneur participating in a competitive market, price elasticity of the demand for his products is infinite. His main weapon in the struggle to expand his field of action consists of offering the goods at a price lower than that prevailing on the market at a given moment. This principle was especially true during the initial stages of industrial development, for the producers were in a position of leadership. When the mechanization of the textile industry commenced in England, the supply of woolens initially and of cotton cloth afterwards grew tremendously, but overall demand did not expand enough to absorb the entire increase in production. A protracted period of sharply declining prices of textiles then set in, undercutting the entire system of artisan production in England and her colonies and, at a slower rate, in a number of other countries.[2] Thus the dynamism of the Industrial Revolution acted, in its first stages, on the side of supply. The entrepreneur's attention focused on the great task of cutting costs by all possible means and production techniques became the crucial point of the entire economic system. A close bond began to arise between economic processes and experimental science—a bond that has become a fundamental characteristic of Western civilization.

The first stage of industrial development consisted mainly of this revolution in supply and its reflection in a steady decline in the prices of a number of lines of general consumption

---

[2] For data on output and prices of cotton textiles in England from the beginning of the Industrial Revolution onwards, see W. W. Rostow, *The Process of Economic Growth* (Oxford, 1953).

merchandise. It was through the price effect that mechanisms tending to destroy a growing number of segments of the old economic structure based on handicrafts operated. Growth in money income was smaller than that of the real product,[3] but, thanks to the vigorous increase in productivity in the mechanized sector (reflecting increasing returns from the scale of production and technological innovations), the profit rate remained on an attractive level. And as the elastic supply of labor caused by the very disruption of the artisanate prevented any pressure from laborers to increase wages, the fruits of increased productivity not transferred to the consuming public through lower prices could be retained almost in their entirety by the entrepreneur. After the passing of the first stage of development, during which the time-honored economic structures were eroded, the dynamic factors of the industrial economy began to operate simultaneously on both the supply and demand sides. In fact, as physical productivity in the consumer goods industries increased, entrepreneurs in that sector were rewarded by greater profits, which prompted increased demand in the capital goods sector.[4] So long as there was no increase in physical productivity in the latter sector, its profit level remained higher than that of the economy as a whole, stimulating a relative increase in investment therein. This relative increase in the demand for capital goods led to an acceleration in growth. Until there was an increase in productivity in the capital goods sector, the expansion of its con-

---

[3] In other words, it was lower than the real product in the monetary sector of the economy due to decline in the price level. However, as the breakdown of the artisan system also implied substitution of subsistence activities by activities integrated into the market, money income on that very account grew more than the real product.

[4] To put this mechanism in an abstract formulation: Whenever there is a reduction in costs in consumer goods industries and hence an increased profit level in that sector, the demand originating in that sector for equipment to expand production capacity leads to increased demand in the capital goods sector.

stituent ensemble of enterprises occurred through absorption of labor. No obstacles impeded this process; indeed, it was favored by the prior increase in physical productivity in the consumer goods sector and consequent release of labor there. Beyond this, expanded employment in the capital goods industry further spurred increased demand for consumer goods. This additional modification in the volume and structure of demand once again affected the direction of investments, now to the benefit of the consumer goods industries. We see here an essential characteristic of early industrialization: in the whole of the process the dynamic impetus, in terms of final consumer goods, arises alternately on both the supply and the demand side of the market.

The model of economic development outlined above refers to mechanisms typical during the phase of Industrial Revolution, the purest instance of which occurred in England. After a considerable period of intense commercial development which engendered substantial colonial expansion and consequent tendencies towards warfare when the lines of trade approached saturation, the problem of costs of production became a factor of greater and greater importance in the economic field. As early as the first half of the eighteenth century, the most advanced technical procedures were keenly coveted and became the object of espionage activities in all countries.[5] Attempts were made to lure men with greater technical experience, by every kind of enticement. Thus the extensive form of growth of the mercantilistic era, aimed at opening up new trade fronts even at the cost of violence, gave way to a new type of growth in depth, whose dynamic force was due to the inner transformations of the economic system. These transformations, however, were not erratic. The progress of

---

[5] Regarding espionage missions sent by the British to the Continent, especially Italy, to copy the most advanced textile equipment, see Paul Mantoux, *The Industrial Revolution in the Eighteenth Century* (London, 1928).

science received a tremendous impulse on all fronts, just as did the application of scientific principles to production techniques. As a result of this, a continuously increasing array of technical innovations came into existence, and the economic feasibility of these new production forms depended on the judgement of the entrepreneurs. To the extent that conditions justified, the new techniques were to become incorporated into production processes. But although the advancement of science and technique became increasingly autonomous—expanding the spectrum of technological potentialities—the economic conditions in each case and in each phase, determined what type of technology was to be employed.

In the first phase of development, before the absorption of the pre-capitalistic system has progressed substantially, the wages of unskilled labor remain basically at a mere subsistence level. Subsequent increasing disruption of the artisan system and consequent increased supply of labor in the urban zones favor a fall rather than a rise in wages.[6] In a general sense, however, it may be said that development took place under conditions of entirely elastic labor supply and with a constant level of real wages in terms of foodstuffs. As the prices of manufactures, measured precisely in terms of food, were on the decline[7] (in fact, but for this fall in prices it would not have been possible to eliminate handicraft production through competition), it may be concluded that wages should display a certain tendency to rise relative to manufactured goods, a circumstance obviously contributing to expansion in demand for manufactured goods in the urban zones. Under these conditions, it cannot be denied that technological innovations were increasingly economical as they afforded greater cost

---

[6] For a recent reconsideration of this circumstance, see E. J. Hobsbawm, "The British Standard of Living 1790-1850," *The Economic History*, August, 1957.

[7] The average prices of cotton textiles produced in England fell some 80 per cent from 1790-1800 to 1840-1850. See Rostow, *op. cit.*, Appendix II.

reduction through increases in production per unit of capital. Up to the middle of the nineteenth century, the capital goods industry—except in the case of the building materials sector—was of relatively minor importance. The volume of investment in the industrial sector was limited far more by the real supply of equipment than by other factors of a strictly economic nature. Equipment was produced on a semi-handicraft basis, and concern with limited costs remained secondary. It was necessary for the equipment industry to achieve a certain degree of maturity and for supply to become relatively elastic in this sector before problems of selective technique began to be conceived in strictly economic terms.

With an elastic supply of labor and ignoring foreign trade for purposes of simplicity, the main factor determining the rate of economic growth is the production capacity of the capital goods industry. The share of the capital goods industry in aggregate production reflects the form of income distribution: the larger this share the greater the share of profit (especially industrial profit) in the aggregate income.[8] Actually, if it is assumed that the consumption of the higher income groups is regulated by institutional factors and is little affected by short-term alterations in the level of aggregate income, and that the consumption of wage earners is determined by the level of their current income and that their saving capacity is almost nil, then it appears that the maximum real consumption of the wage-earning class is determined jointly by the aggregate supply of consumption goods and services and by the level of consumption of the non-wage-earning classes. If for the sake of simplicity we also reason in terms of a closed economy, we find, *ipso facto*, that aggregate supply of consumption goods and services is determined by their own level of production. As the production of consumption goods and capital goods are mutually complementary, a relative increase

---

[8] For an analysis of this point, see N. Kaldor, "Alternative Theories of Distribution," *Review of Economic Studies,* March, 1956.

in one necessarily implies a relative reduction in the other. When workers from the consumer goods sector shift to the capital goods sector, the supply of consumer goods is reduced; but demand remains at a constant level if the shift occurs without any change in average wages. If the average wage increases in order to induce workers to change from one sector to another, it prompts expansion in the demand for consumer goods at the same time that the supply on the market is reduced. In practice, this situation tends to entail a rise in the prices of consumer goods, reduction in average real wages, and hence an increase in the proportion of profit in the product. Thus, if we bear in mind that the output of capital goods has to be purchased by the entrepreneurs with a part of their profits and that the consumption of the non-wage-earning class is stable on a short-term basis, we can reasonably conclude that reduction in the output of consumer goods will cause a reduction in average real wages as well, while increased output of capital goods will result in increased profits. Any of these phenomena will produce alterations in the distribution of income, causing reactions by the interested social groups. It is their attitudes that ultimately determine the form of distribution of income and the structure of production.

The first phase of industrial development, then, features a substantial increase in the participation of the capital goods industry—especially the equipment industry—in aggregate industrial output. This modification in the structure of the production setup is probably accompanied by changes in income distribution, with the total mass of profit growing more intensively than payrolls. It would not be easy to specify when this first stage of industrial development ends; but it is fairly clear that the complete absorption of the pre-capitalistic economy and consequent absorption of the structural labor surplus coincides with the end of that phase. From then on, the supply of labor becomes less elastic and the bargaining position of the working class improves, creating serious obstacles to the absorption of the great mass of capital goods constantly being produced. Such a situation clearly developed in England at the beginning of the last quarter of the nineteenth century. Use of the large and growing volume of capital goods required transfer of labor from that sector to the consumer goods sector, which seems to have caused a relative reduction in the output of capital goods and a redistribution of income in favor of the wage earner. This tendency led to a reduction in the rate of growth and a decline in the rate of profit. The British economy succeeded in avoiding premature euthanasia by launching a great international offensive. This sufficed to initiate the phase of complete liberalization of British trade, of massive capital exports which kept the equipment industry operating to capacity, and of the commercial offensive of the bold Victorian imperialism.

The second phase of the development of industrial economies—when the supply of labor becomes less elastic—is marked by a basic disequilibrium between the capacity for producing capital goods and the possibility of absorbing them. This circumstance arises when the supply of savings tends to grow faster than the labor supply, creating strong pressure for redistribution of income in favor of the workers. Redistribution, however, leads to a decline in the rate of profit, unleashing in turn a series of reactions tending to reduce the volume of investment, to create temporary unemployment, to reduce the rate of economic growth, and so on. The crucial point of the problem therefore lies in the relative inelasticity of the labor supply. Either there must be greater elasticity of the labor supply or a reduction must be effected in the relative volume of production of capital goods, permitting a concomitant redistribution of income in favor of the wage-earning groups. That the capitalist economies have succeeded in solving this problem while maintaining the share of profit in the aggregate income is responsible for perpetuating a high rate of growth in the second stage of modern industrial development. The phase of heavy exports of capital goods at the end of the past and beginning of the present century was a mere transitional period which acquired large proportions only in the case of the first country to industrialize, England. That transition had the merit of permitting refinement of more enduring solutions dealing with the technology itself and progressively oriented towards correcting the basic disequilibrium inherited from the previous stage.

A structural surplus of supply in the capital goods sector tends to be reflected in a reduction in investment costs in the consumer goods sector wherein the majority of the equipment is used. To the extent that lower-priced equipment penetrates into the consumer goods industries, either for replacement or for expansion, the profit level in that sector tends to increase in relation to the economy as a whole. Now the greater profit level in the consumer goods sector signifies that a larger fraction of the consumer goods produced is not consumed by the workers of this sector but is left free to be consumed in the capital goods sector. As the latter sector is not growing, there is pressure for lower consumer goods prices, which ultimately represent an increase in real wages in terms of commodities produced by the manufacturing sector. The tendency towards higher real wages will have a stronger effect on capital goods industries already operating at a low profit level. The result of this situation is that the more advanced techniques—those with greater capital density per person employed—meet with economic conditions relatively more favorable in industries producing capital goods. And the faster advance of technology in the capital goods industries has basic consequences for other aspects of development of the economy. Since their physical productivity grows more intensively than that of consumer goods industries, the prices of equipment tend to decline relative to those of manufactured consumer goods, producing a trend towards the displacement of labor by equipment in the consumer goods industries. This in turn tends to increase the degree of mechanization throughout the system—that is, to increase the density of fixed capital per person employed. Moreover, the price of equipment relative to manufactured consumer goods (and hence in terms of real wages) drops, greater mechanization does not necessarily imply a reduction in the rate of profit on new capital invested.[9]

The vigorous relative advancement of technology in the capital goods industries made it possible to reconcile the form of income distribution (crystallized during the period of absorption of the pre-capitalist economy) and considerable participation by capital goods industries in the aggregate product with a relatively inelastic labor supply.

Equipment providing substantial increases in physical productivity in the consumer goods industries—the automatic loom, for example—were obtained from the capital goods industries almost without requiring increases in price relative to consumer goods. The consequent rise in real wages created good profit potentials for processes even more advanced technologically. Observing the same phenomenon from another standpoint, it might be said that the technology was oriented to permitting combinations of factors which entailed growing quantities of capital per man employed. Inventions which provided savings in the labor factor (given a particular level of production already achieved) took preference over those affording an increase in the physical productivity of labor without causing a reduction in the demand for the labor factor. Especially in the agricultural sector—the big reservoir of manpower—was a substantial effort made to curtail the demand for labor. Farm mechanization, initiated at the end of the past century, eased the labor market tremendously and made a substantial contribution to the maintenance of a high

---

[9] For a keen analysis of relationships between the degree of mechanization and the choice of technology, see Joan Robinson, *The Accumulation of Capital* (London, 1956).

investment level in economies with an advanced degree of mechanization.

The foregoing discussion reveals the close interdependence between the evolution of technology in industrialized countries and the historic conditions of their economic development. Technology as it exists today, incorporated into industrial equipment, is therefore the result of a slow process of "decantation." This process was influenced fundamentally by specific conditions in particular nations, especially Britain and the United States, which from many points of view comprised a single economic system during the first half of the nineteenth century.[10] To draw up an abstract model of the mechanism of those economies in their current state and ascribe to it universal validity, would be tantamount to producing a reincarnation of *homo oeconomicus*, on whose rudimentary psychology the classicists sought to base fundamental economic laws. The obvious and constantly sharpening disparity between the developed and the underdeveloped economies calls for this problem to be formulated in different terms.

THE UNDERDEVELOPED STRUCTURES

The advent of an industrial nucleus in eighteenth century Europe disrupted the world economy of the time and eventually conditioned later economic development in almost every region in the world. The action of that powerful dynamic nucleus proceeded to operate in three directions. The first marks the line of development in Western Europe, within the structure of the political divisions which had crystallized in the preceding mercantile period. This development, as we

---

[10] For an analysis of the interdependence of economic development in England and the United States in the nineteenth century, see the author's *Formação Econômica do Brasil* (Rio de Janeiro, 1959) [also in English: *The Economic Growth of Brazil* (University of California Press, Berkeley and Los Angeles, 1963)], especially Chapter 18.

have seen, was characterized by disorganization of the pre-capitalistic artisan economy and progressive absorption at a higher level of productivity of the factors released. Two phases can be identified in this process: in the first, the release of labor faster than it was absorbed made the supply of this factor wholly elastic; in the second, the tendency towards exhaustion of the labor supply resulting from the disjointing of the pre-capitalistic economy called for reorientation of technology in order to maintain the flexibility of the system so that the factors could be combined in proportions compatible with their respective supplies. Thus the development of technology—the transformations of the capital goods industries—became more and more conditioned by the relative availability of factors in the industrial centers.

The second line of development of the European industrial economy consisted of displacement of frontiers wherever there was still unoccupied land with characteristics similar to those in Europe itself. A number of factors were involved that expansion. In the case of Australia and the American West, gold played a basic role. The revolution in maritime transportation, making it possible to bring grain great distances to compete in the European market, was decisive in other cases. It must be remembered, however, that this displacement of the frontier was not basically different from the process of development of Europe itself, of which it formed a part; the Australian, Canadian, and American economies in that phase were mere extensions, so to speak, of the European industrial economy. The populations which emigrated to those areas took with them European techniques and consumption habits, and on encountering a greater abundance of natural resources they rapidly achieved rather high levels of productivity and income. If we consider that these "colonies" were established only where exceptionally favorable economic potentials existed, we see why their populations achieved right from the start high standards of living relative to those of the European countries.

The third line of expansion of the European industrial economy was towards already inhabited regions, some of which were densely populated, whose old economic systems were of various, but invariably pre-capitalistic types. The contacts between the vigorous capitalistic economies and these regions of long-standing habitation did not occur in a uniform manner. In some cases interest was limited to the opening up of lines of trade. In others there prevailed right from the start a desire to encourage the production of raw materials for which demand was increasing in the industrial centers. The effect of the impact of capitalist expansion on the archaic structures varied from region to region, being conditioned by local circumstances, the type of capitalistic penetration, and the intensity of the penetration. The result, however, was almost always to create hybrid structures, part tending to behave as a capitalistic system, part perpetuating the features of the previously existing system. The phenomenon of underdevelopment today is precisely a matter of this type of dualistic economy.

Underdevelopment is, then, discrete historical process through which economies that have already achieved a high level of development have not necessarily passed. To grasp the essence of the problem of contemporary underdeveloped economies this peculiarity must be taken into consideration. Let us, for example, view the typical instance of an economy into which a capitalistic "wedge" is introduced—let us say productive activities intended for export, a mining undertaking controlled by a capitalistic enterprise which organizes not only production but also marketing of the product. The intensity of the impact of this nucleus on the old structure will depend basically on the relative importance of the income to which it gives rise and which remains available within the community. Thus the impact depends on the volume of labor the enterprise absorbs, the level of the average real wages it offers, and the total amount of taxes it pays. This last item is typically of minor importance during the initial stages of capitalistic expansion, when stimuli of all kinds, including complete tax exemption, are created to attract capital from outside. The level of real wages is determined by living conditions prevailing in the region in which the new enterprises are set up, without any precise connection with the productivity of labor in the new economic activity. Creation of a highly elastic supply of labor requires only that wages in the capitalistic enterprise be somewhat higher than the average for the region. Hence the decisive factor is the volume of labor absorbed by the capitalistic nucleus. But experience shows that this volume of labor did not usually reach large proportions. In the case of the economies specialized in mining, it hardly amounted to 5 per cent of the working age population. Furthermore, the new enterprises tended to encourage and assist local authorities to carry out sanitation and other health measures resulting in a decline in the death rate and a corresponding increase in the rate of growth of the population. After a certain period, the population had increased enough to reëstablish the ratio of population to resources prevailing in the stage prior to the penetration of the capitalistic enterprise.

The economic structure of the region into which the capitalistic enterprise has penetrated—as in the example above—does not necessarily become modified as a result of that penetration. Only a small fraction of the available labor is absorbed by the alien enterprise; the wages paid to that labor are not determined by the level of productivity of the enterprise but by the living conditions prevailing in the region. And the increase in the rate of growth of the population is quite significant. But, all in all, as the capitalist enterprise's connection with the region in which it has been established is almost exclusively as a wage-generating agency, the payroll must attain a relatively substantial level before modifications occur in the economic structure. The phenomenon seems to resemble that observed in the first phase of development of a capitalist economy, when the previously existing artisan scheme is destroyed and absorbed. The similarity is only apparent, however; the capitalistic enterprise penetrating into a previously inhabited region with an archaic economic structure does not become dynamically linked with the latter, for the mass of profit it generates does not become integrated into the local economy.

The dynamism of the capitalist economy results, in the ultimate analysis, from the role the entrepreneurial class plays in it, especially in its having to utilize reproductively a substantial part of its constantly accruing income. We have already mentioned that the consumption of the capitalist class is determined by institutional factors and is largely independent of short-term fluctuations in the level of aggregate income. Its consumption is unquestionably the most stable factor in the aggregate expenditure of the community. But consumption by wage earners is determined by the aggregate employment level, a circumstance which tends to minimize the role it plays in the process of development. What ensures the dynamism of the capitalist economy is the manner of utilization of the mass of income that reverts to the entrepreneurs and which they put aside as savings. This portion does not become tied in with the region in which the enterprise is located; its utilization depends almost exclusively on conditions prevailing in the economy to which the owners of the capital belong. Let us consider the case of British capital invested in South East Asia in companies producing tea, rubber, or metals. The income those enterprises generate becomes integrated partly into the local economy and partly into the British economy. The part involved in the local economy probably tends to be the larger. However, it is the portion connected with the British economy that establishes the dynamic characteristics of the capitalistic system. As a matter of fact, the mass of savings required by the British economy every year for transformation into productive capacity is derived largely from income of firms located all over the world.

It is because of the circumstances just described that the expansion in international trade in the nineteenth century—an expansion resulting from the industrial development of Europe —did not lead to a spreading of the capitalistic system of production on the same scale. The displacement of the European economic frontier almost always resulted in the formation of hybrid economies in which a capitalistic nucleus, so to speak, existed in a state of "peaceful coëxistence" with an archaic structure; the capitalistic nucleus rarely modified the preëxisting structural conditions but was linked with the local economy merely as a formative element creating a mass of wages. Only when the type of enterprise called for the absorption of a large number of wage earners—as on the tea plantations in Ceylon and the rubber plantations in Burma—did the effect of the capitalistic organization on the local economy become of major importance. If the local labor supply was relatively scarce, as in those two countries, the possibility of an increase in real wages arose early (that tendency could be partially annulled, however—as in the two cases in question —by imports of labor from countries with low living standards). Even so, despite an improvement in living standards, there was no structural modification in the economic system— the basic step required for the creation of a typical capitalistic economy was not taken. When external conditions ceased to permit expansion in the output of tea or rubber in those countries, the situation became one of equilibrium at a level of permanent under-employment of factors, a circumstance inconceivable in a typical capitalistic economy. As wages are determined by the conditions of subsistence—and the profit margin is therefore high—the typical company becomes able to absorb substantial price falls and for that reason the level of employment fluctuates little. Price falls, affecting mainly the profit margin, concentrate their effects on the British income itself, into which the profits of the company are integrated. *Mutatis mutandis*, the recovery in prices and the period of abundance pass almost unnoticed in the country in which the enterprise is located, unless factors of another kind make it advisable to utilize the larger profits for expansion of the business in the region in which they are obtained. The decision in regard to a possible expansion in the business is taken in London; it is made from the British, not the economic, point of view. Thus despite the relative strength of the capitalistic nuclei in economies such as that of Ceylon or the Central American countries, these regions have remained essentially pre-capitalistic structures.

But it would be incorrect to conclude that the hybrid economies we have been discussing have behaved in all circumstances as if they were pre-capitalistic structures. In many cases—Brazil is a good example of this—the mass of wages in the sector connected with the international market has been sufficiently large to give a monetary character to an important sector of the economic system. The growth of the monetary sector has prompted substantial modifications in consumption habits, spurred by and spurring the introduction and spread of innumerable articles manufactured abroad. Diversification in consumption habits has had important consequences on the subsequent development of the economy. We have already seen that the level of employment in an economy of this type tends to be relatively stable, even though the value of exports fluctuates in line with the oscillations in international prices for raw materials. Stability in the internal monetary income, by comparison with the instability of importing capacity, creates strong pressure against the balance of payments in phases of declining international prices, and makes it hard to adopt the rules of the gold standard. To the extent that the relative importance of money income within the

Brazilian economy grew because of expansion of the sector connected with the international market, there was a tendency towards increased pressure against the balance of payments during phases of falling international prices. Thus conditions arose favorable to the establishment of activities connected with the domestic market itself, for during phases of strong decline in export prices the profitability of business connected with the domestic market tends to increase in relative terms, inasmuch as the prices of imported commodities rise while the level of money income remains steady.

When exporting activity was partially controlled by national capital—as was the case in Brazil during the period of coffee expansion—the problem presented other important aspects. The mere existence of a large mass of profit formed in activities connected with the external market both opened up new possibilities and created new problems. It must be borne in mind that those profits did not play the same role in the coffee economy that profit plays in an industrial economy. The dynamic factor of the Brazilian coffee economy was external demand, not volume of investment within the coffee sector. If such investments were found to be excessive, the ultimate effect might be a loss of real income through declines in the coffee prices. In the Central American republics two phenomena may be observed side by side, namely: the effect of "incrustation" of foreign companies, as in the banana plantations; and the effects of an expansion partially controlled by national capital, as in the coffee plantations. The results were not much different, although coffee gave rise to a flow of profit over and above that of wages. The profit flow from coffee was reïnvested in the coffee economy itself to the extent that land and labor availabilities permitted. Once possibilities of expansion of the coffee sector had been exhausted, however, the new capital formed therein tended to emigrate rather than look for new fields of application within the system itself.

Brazil's experience, in view of its considerable magnitude,

constitutes a special case. Actually, in view of the great abundance of land suitable for coffee planting and the elasticity of labor supply,[11] investments in coffee growing were not limited by factor availability. This explains why ever since the end of the nineteenth century the situation has been one of chronic over-supply while at the same time it was possible to control supply artificially. During phases of prosperity, the profit in the coffee sector tended to concentrate in that same sector without playing any basic role in altering the structure of the system. The only difference from the situation in Central America lay in the fact that, since there was an elastic factor supply, profit was invested in the same sector that generated it. Voluminous investments in the coffee sector—even when their real profitability was relatively low—led to the absorption of the previously existing subsistence economy and financed European immigration, thus promoting expansion of the monetary sector within the economy. As the requirements for manufactured goods within this sector were fairly high, a market for manufactured products arose which was later to justify the creation of an industrial nucleus which eventually induced a structural transformation in the economy.

The dynamic element in the first stage of European industrial development acted, as we have seen, on the side of supply. Entrepreneurial action—through the introduction of new combinations of factors—created its own demand as it became possible to offer a cheaper and more abundant product. In the case of development induced from without—as in Brazil—the first consequence was a demand for manufactured

---

[11] The first phase of great coffee expansion in Brazil (in the third quarter of the nineteenth century) was based on labor which had remained semi-utilized in the mining region after the gold economy entered into a state of decadence; in the second stage of expansion (last quarter of the past century) the problem of labor was solved by European immigration; the expansion in the 'twenties, 'forties, and 'fifties of this century was based on the absorption of excess labor coming from Minas Gerais and the states in the Northeast.

goods. At first this was met by imports; but the dynamic factor began to act internally, here on the side of demand, from the moment demand could not be met by external supply. On the one hand, the stability in the level of money income, and on the other, instability in importing capacity, acted cumulatively to guarantee attractive conditions for investments linked with the domestic market.[12]

The industrial nucleus based on demand for manufactured goods formerly met out of imports commenced with light industries producing general consumption articles such as textiles and processed foodstuffs. Thus three sectors came to coëxist within the economy: one was the "remnant" economy with a predominance of subsistence activities and a minor money flow; the second comprised activities directly connected with foreign trade; the third consisted of activities connected with the domestic market for general consumption manufactured products. The total constituted an economic structure a good deal more complex than that of mere coëxistence of foreign firms along with the vestiges of a pre-capitalistic system.

In the more simple underdeveloped structures, the mass of wages generated in the exporting sector is the only dynamic element; expansion of the exporting sector engenders a greater flow of money income permitting absorption of factors previously engaged in the subsistence sector; if the exporting sector remains stationary, growth in population brings an enforced reduction in the average real wage level and a decline in the income per inhabitant. In the more complex underdeveloped

---

[12] The policy of artificial control of the supply of coffee introduced in the first decade of this century gave greater stability to importing capacity and very probably had a negative effect on the development of the industrial nucleus already in course of formation. Paradoxically, however, even the "negative" effects of this policy were in at least one situation structurally important: by intensifying and extending the coffee crisis which commenced in 1929 the policy precipitated notable structural transformations.

structures, in which there is an industrial nucleus linked with the domestic market, cumulative reactions may arise tending to cause structural transformations in the system. The basic dynamic factor continues to be external demand; but an important difference lies in its impact: its action is multiplied internally. As external induction increases monetary income, the profit of the industrial nucleus linked with the domestic market also grows; increased investment within that nucleus follows, increasing further the level of money income. All in all, the relative importance of the subsistence sector shrinks, even though the expansion of the external sector is accompanied by an improvement in importing capacity and the competitive power of imports in these phases, reducing the real magnitude of the domestic income multiplier.

The greatest difference occurs, however, in the following stage of contraction of importing capacity, with the decline in the prices of exported products. As money income remains at a relatively high level, the decline in importing capacity causes substantial exchange devaluation. The nucleus thus enters into a boom, precisely during the phase of decline in profitability of the export sector. Although the level of money income declines, exchange devaluation spurs an increase in the demand for domestically produced manufactured goods, and the sector connected with the domestic market shows an improved profit picture. The effective possibilities of growth are partially frustrated, however, by the reduction in importing capacity. High profitability in the industries connected with the domestic market is partly illusory, inasmuch as the cost of replacement of imported equipment increases with exchange devaluation. The existence during a period of relative increase in prices of industrial equipment of a substantial mass of profit due to activities connected with the domestic market gives rise to a tendency to invest capital in activities less dependent on imports, such as the building industry. As these investments do not cause permanent changes in the employment structure of the community, the relative increase tends in the last resort to put a brake on the process of growth itself.

The higher stage in underdevelopment is reached when the industrial nucleus becomes diversified and able to produce part of the equipment needed for expansion of productive capacity. Reaching this stage does not imply that the industrial nucleus connected with the domestic market automatically becomes the main dynamic element. The normal process of development of the industrial nucleus remains a matter mostly of replacement of imports; the dynamic element continues to reside in previously existing demand created mainly by external induction, and not, as in the fully developed industrial économies, in the innovations introduced into the productive processes. But with the system capable of producing a part of the capital goods required for expansion of productive capacity, the process of growth may continue for a far longer time, even if importing capacity is choked off. Under such conditions, for a series of reasons to be commented on at greater length in the next chapter, development takes place with strong inflationary pressure.

We see, then, that underdevelopment is not a necessary stage in the process of formation of the modern capitalistic economies. It is a special process due to the penetration of modern capitalistic enterprises into archaic structures. The phenomenon of underdevelopment occurs in a number of forms and in various stages. The simplest case is that of coëxistence of foreign companies producing export commodities alongside a wide range of subsistence activities. This coëxistence may continue in a state of static equilibrium for long periods. The most complex situation, as in the Brazilian economy at the present time, is that in which there are three sectors in the economy: a subsistence structure, a structure oriented mainly towards export, and an industrial nucleus connected with the domestic market and sufficiently diversified to produce a part of the capital goods it needs for its own growth. The industrial nucleus linked with the domestic market develops through a process of displacing importation of manufactured goods, that is, under permanent competitive conditions with external producers. The greatest concern of the local industrialist is therefore to provide an article similar to the one imported and, consequently, to adopt production methods which make it possible to compete with the foreign producer. In other words, the price structure in the industrial sector connected with the domestic market tends to be similar to that prevailing in highly industrialized countries exporting manufactured goods. Thus the technological innovations which appear most advantageous are those making it possible to approach the cost and price structure of the countries exporting manufactured goods, and not those permitting faster transformation in the economic structure through absorption of the subsistence sector. The practical result of this (even if the industrial sector connected with the domestic market grows and increases its participation in the product and even if the per capita income of the population as a whole rises) is that the occupational structure of the country changes only slowly. The part of the population affected by development remains minor, and there is a very slow decline in the relative importance of the sector whose main activity is production for subsistence. This explains why an economy in which industrial production has already achieved a high degree of diversification—with the share of the industrial sector in the product hardly distinguishable from that in more highly developed countries—may present a rather pre-capitalistic occupational structure and have a large portion of its population cut off from the benefits of development.

Again we see that underdevelopment, specific phenomenon that it is, calls for an effort at autonomous theorization. Lack of such an effort has led many economists to explain by analogy with the experience in developed economies problems which can be properly expressed only through full understanding of the phenomenon of underdevelopment. The tendency in countries with an underdeveloped economy, such as Brazil, towards disequilibrium in the balance of payments is one of those which, for lack of a proper theoretical basis, has most commonly been incorrectly presented and misinterpreted.

5 : *External Disequilibrium in Underdeveloped Structures*

STRUCTURAL CAUSES OF DISEQUILIBRIUM

In line with the concept sketched out in the preceding chapter, we may define an underdeveloped structure as one in which full utilization of available capital is not a sufficient condition for complete absorption of the working force at a level of productivity corresponding to the technology prevailing in the dynamic sector of the system. What basically characterizes underdevelopment is the technological heterogeneity of the various sectors of the total economy. According to current economic theory, mobility of factors and flexibility of production coefficients ought to preclude great extremes of technological diversity.[1] But the applicability of this theoretical scheme—with its implicit homogeneous and linear production functions—is really quite limited. It applies only in those situations in which there is entrepreneurial option among technologies providing a wide gamut of combinations of factors. From the point of view of the entrepreneur in an underdevel-

---

[1] For a discussion of this point within the context of the marginal theory, see "A análise marginalista e a teoria do subdesenvolvimento," in *Contribuições à Análise do Desenvolvimento Econômico* (Essays in honor of Eugênio Gudin) (Rio de Janerio, 1957).

oped country, technology assumes the character of an independent variable, inasmuch as the equipment is imported from highly industrialized countries; moreover, the very form of development of the industrial sector of an underdeveloped economy—the process of substitution of imports—leads the entrepreneur to adopt a technology compatible with a cost and price structure similar to that prevailing in the international manufactured goods market. As we have noted, this circumstance arises because underdevelopment evolves not as an endogenous transformation of a pre-capitalistic economy but from a process of grafting onto the latter one or more enterprises connected with the commercial activity of industrialized economies in a state of expansion. The misunderstanding of traditional economics in this respect is due to a failure to realize that development by external induction is different from the classic formation process of the European capitalistic economies.

If we view underdevelopment as a state of factor unbalance reflecting a lack of adjustment between the availability of factors and the technology of their use, so that it is impossible to achieve full utilization of both capital and labor simultaneously, we also come to recognize that underdeveloped structures are hybrid systems consisting of sectors each with a specific type of behavior. Following in the schematic representation of such systems introduced earlier, we call the developed sector, in which modern technology predominates, the nucleus, whether it produces for the external or for the domestic market; we refer to the remaining sector of the pre-capitalistic structure as the backward sector. The degree of underdevelopment is a function of the relative importance of the backward sector, and the rate of growth is a function of the increase in the relative importance of the developed sector.[2] The intensity of this increase depends on the rate of

---

[2] For a strict definition of this point and its mathematical expression, see the author's "The External Disequilibrium in the Underdeveloped Economies," *The Indian Journal of Economics*, April, 1958.

capital formation, the nature of the technology already absorbed, and the rate of population growth in the economy as a whole. A given rate of capital formation might be sufficient for increasing per capita product and yet be insufficient for growth in the relative importance of the developed sector. Actually, if the developed sector increases its product without absorbing new contingents of labor, and if all population growth has to be absorbed by the backward sector at the level of productivity prevailing in that sector, then the rise in per capita income of the total population may not be accompanied by a relative increase in the developed sector. In other words, despite the rise in per capita income, the degree of underdevelopment is not altered comparably.

The structural definition of underdevelopment, as expounded in the preceding paragraph, has a sufficient degree of generality to provide an explanation for a series of cases which do not fit in with the current definitions wherein the level of per capita income, the degree of utilization of natural resources, and so on are taken as a basis. In accordance with our definition, we may classify as totally developed structures even some countries in which there is an obvious under-utilization of natural resources, such as Australia and Canada, and countries which depend upon imports of capital goods for their economic growth, such as New Zealand. This definition also permits us to classify as relatively developed—or at least as having a fairly advanced underdeveloped structure—a nation such as Japan, with a per capita income lower than that of several Latin American countries. Finally, it enables us to demonstrate meaningfully that the degree of development of the Uruguayan economy is higher than that of Puerto Rico— despite the fact that per capita income is of the same order in each, and even than that of Venezuela, whose per capita income is more than 50 per cent greater than that of Uruguay.

Having established that the growth of an underdeveloped economy implies structural modifications, let us see what practical consequences are entailed. The relative increase in the developed sector—let us call it sector A—bringing about the assimilation of more complex production techniques, leads to alterations in the multiple relationships of the various groups of productive activities. Let us take as an example the introduction of such techniques into an agricultural region in which subsistence activities prevail. Before their introduction, monetary income is relatively small; each family produces on its own plot much of the food it needs. The new technology brings with it specialization, production able to compete on the market. The new production methods require—indeed, comprise the use of—more complex agricultural tools, fertilizers, insecticides, weed killers, modern means of storage and transportation, and the like. A complex of relationships is created between the agricultural sector and various activities in other sectors of the productive process, increasing demand for a number of processed or semi-processed goods supplied by the manufacturing sector. What is particularly important is the way in which this transformation takes place. In a developed economy, technological progress takes place gradually: an improvement in farm mechanization methods may lead to substitution of one tractor by another of a more efficient type, cheapening of a certain kind of fertilizer may signify a new use for land previously utilized for extensive stock breeding, and so on. The whole of these gradual modifications have very little effect on the overall structure of relationships constituting the economic system. In the underdeveloped economy, on the other hand, expansion of sector A induces abrupt change for a whole segment of the input structure; the demand for manufactured and semi-manufactured goods increases suddenly. The transportation sector offers another good example: the change from animal (including human) haulage to motor traction occurs "in one fell swoop." The handicraft-produced cart and locally bred draft livestock are shoved aside by the motorized vehicle; a whole sector of highly advanced industrial processes arises whose operation and maintenance call for a complex input setup.

This manner of growth of the underdeveloped countries—featured by sharp increase in the demand for intermediate products of industrial origin—leads to a tendency for an increase in the import coefficient. The problem can be presented simply in a numerical model. Let us suppose the process of growth takes the form of a manpower transfer from backward sector B to advanced sector A. We assume that the advanced level of technology predominating in sector A is in a stationary condition—that is, growth occurs by the addition of new units of the same type as those already in existence. Hence there is no release of labor from sector A, whose expansion depends on the transfer of manpower. Such a situation is similar, in a number of aspects, to that of a country whose expansion is based on imported manpower, without significant technological innovations, as occurred with the displacement of the coffee frontier on the São Paulo plateau during the last two decades of the nineteenth century. In this type of situation labor immigrates not from another country but from another region of the country itself or from another sector of the economy. Within this situation, average productivity in each individual sector remains stationary; but since productivity is higher in A than in B, the manpower transfer from B to A results in an increase in the average productivity of the economy as a whole. If we furthermore assume in our numerical example that in the initial stage 20 per cent of the labor force had already been absorbed by sector A, whose average productivity was five times as high as that of sector B, we may readily compute that sector A accounted for 55 per cent of the product (and income) of the whole economy. Let us assume now that the import coefficient is 0.4 in sector A and only 0.1 in sector B, something perfectly explainable in the light of the differences between production processes and the greater diversification in consumption habits of the population in the developed sector. If we assign arbitrary numerical values, get the following structure for total supply during the initial period:

Sectors	Aggregate product and expenditure	Imports	Production for the domestic market
A	100	40	60
B	80	8	72
Total	180	48	132

This model assumes that there are no transfers of income between the two sectors and that imports in each equal exports, or, to put it another way, that there is no transfer of exchange between A and B. The average import coefficient, as may be computed, is 0.27.

Starting from this initial situation, we now allow for net investments to be concentrated in sector A and assume that in the course of period of time sector A increases its use of labor by 50 per cent, raising its participation in the total labor force from 20 to 30 per cent. Since productivity in A is five times as high as in B, this transfer of labor entails an increase of 22 per cent in the total product, which rises from 180 to 220. Although sector B still has 70 per cent of the labor force, it provides only 32 per cent of the product. If we assume that the respective import coefficients of the two sectors are maintained, the practical consequence in this area is an increase of 39 per cent in the import quantum, raising the average coefficient from 0.27 to 0.31. Thus an increase of 22 per cent in the product is matched by an increase of 32 per cent in the demand for imports. Thus the position at the end of the period in question is as follows:

Sectors	Aggregate product and expenditure	Imports	Production for the domestic market
A	150	60	90
B	70	7	63
Total	220	67	153

Obviously the situation demonstrated in the numerical example given above would be conceivable only if production for foreign markets expanded with greater intensity than that for the domestic market. It is the typical instance of an economic system that develops by increasing exports, as occurred with the coffee economy in Brazil, the sugar economy in Cuba, and so on. We can, however, accept this instance as exemplifying a position *ex ante* required by the dynamics of growth in an underdeveloped economy, and which comes into being only when favorable conditions of the balance of payments permit. In the preliminary phases of underdevelopment —with prevalence of external dynamic impulse and existence of a low income multiplier—the tendency to a rise in the import coefficient does not create any major difficulties. It is in the intermediate and higher stages of transformation of underdeveloped structures that the problem achieves full relevance, for when the external impulse is internally amplified or when an autonomous domestic impulse arises strong pressure against the balance of payments almost always makes itself felt.

The numerical model presented, insofar as it refers to an *ex post* situation, is indicative of a growth process induced from without. A typical instance of this is the case of growth rise, the effects on the real income in sector A are concentrated in the profits of production and commerce, forthwith providing a stimulus to increased investments in the sector, with transfer of labor from sector B. Inasmuch as the initial impulse comes from without, the first phase of the process is characterized by a rise in importing capacity, such rise being far larger in relative terms than that of the real income.

Starting from the initial position given in the preceding numerical example, let us assume that improvement in prices increases the value of exports from 40 to 50 in sector A; the immediate rise in income is from 100 to 110. The increment in the former case is 25 per cent; in the latter, the increment is only 10 per cent. Reasoning in comparative static terms— and supposing that in the initial and final positions the net investments are equal to zero—it can easily be shown that, if the same parameters are maintained, the demand for imports could hardly exceed importing capacity. Actually, even if the entire increase in income were invested, it would be necessary for the ratio of marginal output to capital to exceed 1.5 for import demand to rise more than 25 per cent—that is, to produce disequilibrium in the balance of payments.[3] As a ratio of 1.5 is inconceivable for all practical purposes—excluding the hypothesis of a situation of gross unemployment in the initial position—it may be asserted that in the case in question the tendency will be towards the formation of surplus importing capacity—in other terms, accumulation of exchange reserves.

This comparison between two static situations is, however, entirely artificial. Even assuming that in the initial position the level of net investment equals zero, it is inconceivable that the effects of an improvement in the terms of trade would become exhausted in one production period. If this improvement lasts for a certain period of time, the least that can be expected is that the volume of net investment induced thereby will be maintained. If so, income will increase from 100 to 110 during the first period, and net investments from 0 to 10. Let us assume that this volume of net investment creates in the following period additional productive capacity of the order of 5—making it possible to achieve an income volume of 115—that, in other words, the output:capital ratio is 0.5. If in successive periods the same volume of net investment (10) and the same output:capital ratio obtain, the annual increase in income will be constant (5), and hence decreasing in relative terms. At the end of the fifth period, income in sector A will have increased from 100 to 130 and the demand for imports will have increased from 40 to 52, or, to put it another way, above the initial growth in import capacity. To conceive of this type of disequilibrium, one would have to assume,

---

[3] A marginal output:capital ratio of 1.5 would mean that the value of the rise in income is 50 per cent higher than the value of the increase in productive capacity.

however, that growth in sector A is based exclusively on the domestic market itself, which is obviously improbable. As the improvement in export prices increased the relative profitability in the sector producing for the external market, investment connected with this market would in all likelihood expand. Thus if a decline in export prices is excluded by hypothesis, importing capacity must grow more than the increase permitted by the improvement in the terms of trade.

In the example given in the preceding paragraph, we have assumed the volume of net investments would remain constant and that there would therefore be a persistent decline in the rate of growth. A situation of this type could hardly occur in an underdeveloped economy that had already achieved the intermediate and higher stages to which we have referred above. As a matter of fact, in underdeveloped economies that have achieved some degree of diversification in their production structures, a dynamic impulse—either from without or from within the economy itself—does induce a stage of accelerated growth. There is, in other words, an increase in the rate of investment. In the case of an improvement in terms of trade, the greater profitability of the export sector is reflected not only directly in investments within its own field but also indirectly in such fields as transportation and other services. The domestic capital goods industry thus receives an impulse amplified by the well known mechanism of the accelerator. On the other hand, the increase in the level of income available for consumption has an immediate effect on the demand for manufactured goods, whose income elasticity in the underdeveloped countries, as is well known, is greater than one. If the greater demand for manufactured consumer goods is faced with a somewhat inelastic supply, the result is a rise in relative prices in that sector, with increased profitability and intensified investment, which provide an additional impulse to the capital goods industry.

All these reactions tending to increase investment stand out even more clearly when the dynamic impulse is the result of internal action. If, for example, the government reorients its expenditures, curtailing current spending so that investments increase without augmenting the fiscal burden, and if the rise in the product due to this higher investment is likewise guided towards capital formation, then the economy will enter into a stage of hastened growth which will be exhausted only when the investment rate becomes stabilized again. Such a speed-up in growth—whether due to a fortuitous conjunction of favorable factors or to deliberate action on the part of the central authorities—causes a series of structural changes which, in an underdeveloped economy, tend to raise the import coefficient. (A simplified model demonstrates this process below, page 153.)

It is a general characteristic of underdeveloped economies that their capital formation processes depend greatly on foreign trade. This dependency occurs not only in connection with the formation of savings but mainly in regard to the transformation of savings into real investments. In the initial stages of underdevelopment, this dependency is quite marked, with emphasis on the savings angle and relatively little effect on real investment, at least in economies expanding through displacement of an agricultural frontier, as was the case with coffee in Brazil, when investment is aimed mainly at the opening up of land, forming of new plantations, rural construction, and so on. Except in the transportation sector, little foreign exchange expenditure is required, and it is altogether probable that the import coefficient of the consuming sector is the same as or higher than that in the investment sector. An indirect indication of this circumstance is to be found in the composition of Brazilian imports during the first few years of the present century, when foodstuffs and textiles accounted for about half the total value involved. Imports of capital goods at that time emphasized building materials and transportation

equipment. As the economic structure passed into the intermediate and higher stages of underdevelopment, the situation
underwent various changes. As a matter of fact, it was now
not so much from the angle of savings that the capital formation process was linked with the external sector, since
profitability in the sector producing for the domestic market—
at least as regards the industrial nucleus—was not always unfavorable by comparison with that of the external sector,
whereas the relative profits obtained in the industrial sector
might be even higher. On the other hand, while the formation
of savings becomes less dependent on the export sector, it is
almost always accompanied in the intermediate phases of
underdevelopment by greater dependency in the transformation of savings into real capital. The expansion of production
capacity no longer takes place by mere accretion of new land
or further expansion of plantations; instead, the relative importance of industry and related services grows, and intensification in the density of mechanical equipment becomes
salient in the capital formation process. Furthermore, the
growing urbanization which goes along with industrialization
calls for transformations in the building industry. Locally produced materials made by semi-handicraft techniques give way
to others whose manufacture requires a high density of
mechanical equipment, such as cement and structural steel.
Thus in the building industry too there is a tendency towards
a rise in the import coefficient.

Brazil's experience in the recent past indicates that, for an
import coefficient of about 10 per cent in the economy as a
whole, participation of imports in the value of net investments
amounts to about a third, which leads to a coefficient more
than three times as high as the average. Furthermore, if we
single out from among the investments those actually creating
productive capacity, then the need for exchange cover rises to
about two thirds. In other words, the import coefficient

(higher than 0.6) is nearly ten times as high as that in the consumption sector.[4] It is this great difference between the coefficient of import in the investment sector and that in the consumption sector that accounts for the tendency to increased pressure on the balance of payments whenever favorable circumstances permit intensification in the rate of growth. This can be seen in quantitative terms from the following numerical model (see facing page).

Case I is an instance of an underdeveloped structure whose import coefficient in the initial phase is 0.148 (14.8 per cent). If we observe the total expenditure closely, we see that the capital goods sector demands a relatively larger volume of imports. Actually, if 14.8 per cent of the total planned expenditure corresponds to the demand for imports, that percentage represents only 10.0 in the consumption sector whereas in the investment sector it amounts to 50.0. The model also shows a rate of investment of 12.0 per cent and an output:capital ratio 0.5, inasmuch as a net investment of 6 in the first period leads to an increase of 3 in the product in the succeeding period. The depreciation rate is 0.03 of the real capital, or 6 per cent of the gross product, equal to half that capital, as is implicit from the output:capital ratio of 0.5.

In view of the parameters and relationships established in the model, we shall assume that the objective of a development policy might lie in raising the investment rate from 12 to 16 per cent of the gross product over a three-year period. The reflection of this effort on the import coefficient can be seen in the numerical example given. While the gross product (and planned expenditure) grows from 100.0 to 112.0, the demand for imports increases from 14.8 to 18.4, increments of 12.0 and 24.3 per cent respectively. The rise in demand for imports at a rate twice as high as that for the increase in aggregate demand reflects structural modifications spurred by

---

[4] For the basic data, see *O Desenvolvimento Econômico do Brasil* (ECLA Mixed Group, Rio de Janeiro, 1956).

BEHAVIOR OF THE IMPORT COEFFICIENT IN A PHASE OF ACCELERATED DEVELOPMENT, IN UNDERDEVELOPED (I) AND DEVELOPED (II) STRUCTURES.

| Period | Investments | | | Gross product | Consumption | Imports | | | Investment rate | % of imports in aggregate expenditure |
	Depreciation	Net	Total			Capital goods	Consumption goods	Total		
				Type I Structures						
1	6.0	6.0	12.0	100.0	88.0	6.0	8.8	14.8	12.0	14.8
2	6.2	8.2	14.4	103.0	88.6	7.2	8.9	16.1	14.0	15.6
3	6.4	9.7	16.1	107.1	91.0	8.1	9.1	17.2	15.0	16.1
4	6.7	11.2	17.9	112.0	94.1	9.0	9.4	18.4	16.0	16.4
				Type II Structures						
1	6.0	6.0	12.0	100.0	88.0	1.2	13.6	14.8	12.0	14.8
2	6.2	8.2	14.4	103.0	88.6	1.4	13.7	15.1	14.0	14.7
3	6.4	9.7	16.1	107.1	91.0	1.6	14.1	15.7	15.0	14.7
4	6.7	11.2	17.9	112.0	94.1	1.8	14.5	16.3	16.0	14.6

the acceleration in growth. As the investment coefficient goes up, the import coefficient also rises, due directly to the need investment creates for greater exchange coverage.

The contrast presented in case II, referring to a developed economy, is illuminating. This economy, with an identical initial import coefficient, also strives to speed up growth by increasing the investment effort. As in case I, the greater investment effort is made without direct detriment to consumption, and a substantial portion of the increase in product goes into the capital formation effort. The fundamental difference between the two economies lies in the composition of imports: whereas in the first case capital goods represent 40 per cent of the total, in the second they account for only 8 per cent. The practical consequence of this is that acceleration of growth occurs without pressure on the balance of payments, and there is even a slight decline in the import coefficient.

These examples suggest that for a given rate of increase in world trade the rate of growth compatible with internal stability is far higher in developed than in underdeveloped structures. This circumstance explains, on the one hand, the slower growth of underdeveloped economies during the past few decades, and accounts, on the other, for the well known tendency to disequilibrium in the balance of payments observed in all underdeveloped countries which endeavor in one way or another to intensify their rate of growth.

CURRENT MONETARY ANALYSIS OF THE PROBLEM OF DISEQUILIBRIUM

The current method of approaching the problem of external disequilibrium typically starts from a definition of the position of disequilibrium in the balance of payments. This method is simply an extension of the theory of general equilibrium according to which, under particular institutional conditions, the economic system *tends* towards a position in which optimum utilization of resources and factors is achieved, and wherein each factor receives remuneration, in line with its marginal productivity. Economic "normality" is then defined in terms of this theoretical position, and anything implying a departure from it is considered more or less abnormal and transitory. The idea of a "normal pattern," a position of equilibrium, in the balance of payments, implies the assumption that there is a specific exchange rate compatible with both domestic and external equilibrium. This exchange rate should be matched by an optimum level of external trade—that is, a level of exports in which marginal productivity of factors absorbed by the exporting sector is identical with that of the factors utilized in production for the domestic market, and a level of imports such that it is possible to equate marginal productivity of factors producing for export with productivity potentially capable of substituting imports. Hence any modification in the exchange rate would lead to a redistribution of factors between the various sectors, with loss of real income. It is implicit in this theory that different economic structures display a high degree of similarity and that there is an actual possibility of competition in the factor market between producers aiming at the external market and those operating for the domestic market. The latter would therefore be able to compete with the importers.

Although other areas of modern economic analysis have little by little put aside the instrument of general equilibrium,[5] this approach has retained the whole of its vigor as regards the analysis of balance of payments problems. The procedure in this case is oriented by purely empirical criteria: a balance of payments in a state of equilibrium is defined as being one which does not create problems. To quote E. M. Berstein: "A proper balance of payments is one that enables a country, over an average of good years and bad, to meet its payments (includ-

---

[5] On this point, see Joan Robinson, *The Accumulation of Capital* (London, 1956), pp. 57-60.

ing ordinary capital outflow) out of its receipts from current transactions and ordinary capital inflow, without compelling it to keep economic activity below a desirable level or to restrict imports merely for the purpose of avoiding a deficit in its balance of payments."[6] This criterion of normality by reference to a period of "good years and bad" implies that cyclical fluctuations, for which the classic remedy is the moving of reserves, are self-compensatory, and therefore fall within the arena of "normality." The statement that balance of payments equilibrium should be compatible with a "desirable level" of economic activity and that both objectives should be achieved without measures restricting imports is an indirect way of presenting the theory of compatibility between domestic and external equilibrium under conditions of optimum utilization of resources and factors.

This approach to the problem of external disequilibrium has important practical consequences. Once the pattern of normality has been defined the next step is to identify the causes of "departure" from that normality. The method of analysis has an attractive simplicity. The criterion for abnormality is simply that disequilibrium exists whenever the imbalance of payments (positive or negative) tends to exceed some definite limits. Let us suppose, to take a common instance, that the imbalance which is piling up is a negative one. Then the aggregate expenditure of the community—the sum of its consumption expenditures and investments in both private and public sectors—is obviously higher than its real income. If the disequilibrium is due to phenomena which are to some extent provisional—as in the case of crop losses, a cyclical decline in export prices, etc.—then the country affected must be prepared to correct it by liquidation of exchange reserves. If there is persistent disequilibrium due to more fundamental causes, it will be possible to avoid complete loss of reserves

---

[6] *International Monetary Fund Staff Papers*, August, 1956, p. 151.

only if these can be identified. The causes of the persistent disequilibrium may attach either to a decline in exports or to an increase in the demand for imports. Let us consider these two possibilities in turn.

Any reduction in the value of exports derives from a drop in export prices, a contraction in quantities exported, or both together. Whatever the case may be, there is always a reduction in the income generated by the exporting sector of the economy, and this reduction is transmitted to the aggregate income, being duly amplified by the multiplier mechanism. But that same mechanism, while intensifying the initial contraction in the aggregate income, concomitantly reduces the demand for imports, thus contributing to the reëstablishment of a state of equilibrium of the balance of payments. If the demand for imports remains high, it is because autonomous factors have helped maintain monetary income at a high level.

Let us assume, for the sake of argument, that the drop in export prices is cushioned by a subsidy policy ensuring the income level of the export sector. If the subsidies are not financed with resources from abroad, they have to be financed either by internal transfers of income (calling for a reduction of consumption or of investment in other sectors) or by the creation of new means of payment. Transfers of income do not avoid contraction of the aggregate income and therefore do not prevent automatic readjustment of the balance of payments. If readjustment does not occur, the sole explanation is that the subsidy was financed by the creation of new means of payment—that is, in an inflationary manner. Hence it might be concluded in this case that external disequilibrium, strictly speaking, does not result from a contraction in the value of exports but from inflationary expansion of monetary income.

The case of a negative balance due to an increase in imports seems to be even simpler. It is obvious that under these circumstances aggregate expenditure grows faster than the product—the negative balance of payments can be nothing but an excess of the former over the latter. Such an excess indicates that the community has exerted a purchasing power greater than that corresponding to current payments to production factors. What has been imported over and above the product has in effect been financed by means of payment which did not originate in current remuneration to production factors. The means of payment could originate only from a reduction in net assets or from the issuance of new currency by the monetary authority. Thus this is also an inflationary phenomenon.

Inflation, which underlies the disequilibrium in the balance of payments, may not always be a visible phenomenon—it need not always be expressed by an increase in the price level. In the case just described, of a reduction in the value of exports, inflation would merely keep the price level stable. The difference between monetary income and real product is equal to the negative balance on the balance of payments, as defined in the way we have mentioned previously. There being no disequilibrium between the aggregate supply—production for the domestic market "plus" imports—and aggregate expenditure, there would be no reason for any change in the general price level. In the second case, that of an increase in imports, the disequilibrium in the balance of payments shows up precisely when the price level begins to stabilize. Let us assume that there is a situation of full employment, with a fixed exchange rate and freedom to import. An increase in expenditure due to expansion of the means of payment then leads to a gradual rise in the domestic price level. To the extent that this increase actually occurs, and given a fixed exchange rate, the relative prices of imported products continue to decline. The practical consequence will be a gradual rise in the import coefficient. After some lapse of time, the rise in imports will equal the initial increase in monetary income, and the equilibrium between aggregate supply and expenditures will be reëstablished. From that time on there will no longer be a rise in the price level and the sole external sign of disequilibrium will be the negative balance of payments.

Thus if using this approach we consider the problem of external disequilibrium as a persistent phenomenon, we are bound to reach the conclusion that the cause lies in a process of chronic inflation, of disequilibrium of costs and prices resulting from previous inflation repressed but remaining latent. The first case would seem clear. If under conditions of full employment expenditure exceeds value of production and the autonomous factors leading to this disequilibrium operate permanently, balance of payments equilibrium can be achieved only by a continuing decline in the external value of the currency. With a fixed exchange rate, pressure against the balance of payments will occur from two directions. As has been shown, there will be pressure, on the one hand, to increase the import coefficient; on the other, there will be a tendency towards a reduction in exports since their competitive capacity will decline. Reduction in exports is a typical instance of disequilibrium produced by a relative increase in costs and prices. We have seen that if inflationary expansion prevails during merely a limited period of time the rise in the price level tends to reach a limit and the disequilibrium is reflected wholly in a negative balance of payments. In that case, the economy proceeds to operate at a higher level of costs and prices, which may seriously affect its competitive position on foreign markets. Under such conditions, even if it were possible to eliminate the pressure on the balance of payments from the side of import demand (which can be achieved by fiscal measures such as an increase in tariffs), the disequilibrium would still persist, for the cost and price level at which the economy was operating would cause a decline in importing capacity. In the former case, correction of the disequilibrium would call for measures aimed at reducing the level of expenditure; in the latter, for action to correct the external overvaluation of the currency.

In contrast to the preceding cases, in which the external disequilibrium stands out as a typical manifestation of an inflationary process, it is customary to make an exception of individual cases in which structural reasons for disequilibrium are recognized. A classic instance of this existed in Chile, which lost its world monopoly of the industrial source of nitrogen after World War I. Problems of a similar nature appear quite frequently, in various degrees of seriousness, and may create troublesome difficulties for countries specializing in a single export product. However, the opinion of the very champions of the point of view we are presenting is that "structural changes by themselves are not of major significance as causes of balance of payments difficulties."[7]

The formulation set forth in the preceding paragraphs, tending to identify external disequilibria with various forms of inflationary processes, has given rise to practical limitations of definite significance. It leads to identifying external disequilibrium with inflation, for all purposes of economic policy. And as inflation is a problem calling for measures to produce short-term effects, the mere suspicion that disequilibrium might have deeper roots becomes relegated to a secondary plane. A clear sign of this is the inability of the economists connected with the International Monetary Fund to agree on what should be understood by "fundamental disequilibrium" of the balance of payments. The basic document under which the Fund was created refers to this type of disequilibrium without, however, defining it, and the enormous volume of existing literature pertaining to the subject hinges entirely on concepts derived from the formulation referred to above. Instead of going deeper into an analysis of possible causes of disequilibrium—that is, a disproportionate growth of this or that sector of the economy—attention is focused more on the symptoms of disequilibrium and on discussions of what a deficit on the balance of payments is or is not.

---

[7] *Ibid.*, p. 157.

Initially there was a tendency towards a broad approach to the problem. Unfortunately, this was not taken as a starting point for any attempt to achieve greater conceptual precision. J. J. Polak admitted in 1947 that "fundamental disequilibrium" may be due both to modifications in relative prices and to transformations in demand and supply.[8] Within this perspective, it was concluded that any disequilibrium of a persistent kind was "fundamental" by its very nature. At about the same time Triffin advanced a definition which for many years has been widely accepted—that fundamental disequilibrium is "a maladjustment in a country's economy so grave and persistent that the restoration or maintenance of satisfactory levels of domestic activity, employment, and incomes should prove incompatible with equilibrium in the balance of payments if not accompanied by extraordinary measures of external defense, such as a change in the exchange rates, increased tariff or exchange control protection, etc."[9] This definition states, in short, that if an economy has to devaluate the currency, impose exchange controls, or modify tariffs in order to maintain or restore full employment, that economy is afflicted by a fundamental disequilibrium. The consequence of so broad a definition is a tendency to consider fundamental any disequilibrium, without taking into consideration more far-reaching causes which may require measures other than those explicitly suggested in the definition. The structural causes referred to by the Fund's theoreticians—factors which could not be corrected by measures of a monetary nature, such as deflation and devaluation—achieve only superficial reference and remain, as we have mentioned, on a secondary plane. But without a detailed analysis of these causes we shall never go beyond mere description of the external symptoms of the

---

[8] "Exchange Depreciation and International Monetary Stability," *Review of Economic Statistics,* August, 1947, p. 174.

[9] *National Central Banking and the International Economy* (International Monetary Policies, Washington, D.C., 1947).

persistent disequilibria which accompany the structural transformations of the underdeveloped economies.

A REFORMULATION OF THE PROBLEM

The analysis set forth above leads to a conclusion which has
had harmful practical consequences for the underdeveloped
countries. The treatment of external disequilibrium is limited,
in the majority of cases, to the adoption of two easily handled
instruments: deflation and devaluation.[10] Since these two instruments are basically monetary functions, the handling of
the problem becomes exclusively a matter for the monetary
authorities. Hence the complete predominance of criteria of
stability in the realm of balance of payments problems, with
no attention to the interdependence between them and the
structural modifications required by development.

The process of adjustment implicit in the current analysis
of the disequilibria of the balance of payments has as its back-
ground the action of the price effects resulting from devaluation. It is assumed that in the face of a relative rise in the
prices of imported products demand will tend to shift to
domestically produced articles, just as when there is a rise in
prices of exported products factors will tend to shift to export
activities. Adjustments obviously depend on price elasticity
of external supply of these same products. The real gain in
exports also depends on price elasticity of the external demand
for exported products and price elasticity of domestic supply
of those same products. The degree of adjustment will thus
depend upon the way in which these four types of elasticity
operate. It so happens, however, that the theoretical models—
which tend to mix up external disequilibrium and inflationary

---

10 Exceptions to this rule, which are recognized by the experts of the
International Monetary Fund, are presented as uncommon cases and
evoke only passing references. See, for example, Triffin's reference to the
nitrate industry in Chile, in the article quoted, p. 78.

situations with excess of expenditure over product—are always predicated upon a situation of full employment. If we start with such a hypothesis, we also have to assume that on a short-term basis the elasticity of domestic supply is equal to zero, and that it is not possible to increase exports without reducing production substituting for imports, or vice versa. In an under-developed economy, the consequences of devaluation may be quite harmful, as will be explained below.

Let us consider the case of an underdeveloped economy whose exporting sector consists of large international concerns engaged in ore mining. If these firms are operating to capacity, elasticity in export supply on a short-term basis is almost nil. Once devaluation is carried out, there is a rise in the prices of the products exported and the benefits accruing concentrate in the companies' profits. These larger profits will probably be remitted abroad, reducing the supply of exchange for other purposes. An increase in the prices of imports will also occur and, as the possibility of substituting these on a short-term basis is likewise nil, the final result will be a rise in the price level, its size depending upon the share of imports in internal supply. A series of internal transfers of income, especially in favor of the exporting sector, and a loss of real income corresponding to the larger remittances by the foreign companies —such are the results of devaluation.

The adjustment model based on elasticities implies a highly diversified economic structure. If exports are merely the complement of production for the domestic market—as in indus-trialized countries exporting manufactured goods—there is always the possibility of increasing sales abroad, on a short-term basis, by curtailing sales in the domestic market. This will produce a transfer of income to the benefit of industries of larger exporting capacity, which will create conditions for a medium-term reorientation of investments and changes in the economic structure in favor of a higher export coefficient.

In the case of underdeveloped countries, it is significant

that, although exports are hardly diversified at all, each major product is exported in relatively large quantities. Any reduction in prices aimed at boosting exports will therefore mean the loss of a portion of the income produced by exporting at the lower level. If, for instance, Chile were to reduce by 10 per cent the supply price of copper, there would obviously be a need for increasing exports by more than 11 per cent merely to maintain exchange availabilities.[11] Since Chilean exports of copper amount to some 400,000 tons, the increase would have to be more than 44,000 tons, a figure hard to achieve without harming other exporting countries. In cases such as this, it is necessary to bear in mind the price elasticity of the supply from other countries competing in the same market. Inasmuch as most countries exporting raw materials are underdeveloped —and have as a common characteristic high price inelasticity of supply in the export sector—it is understandable that they cannot readily solve balance of payments problems through fast expansion of exports.

Direct deflation as a corrective method of handling external disequilibrium would find immediate justification in the assumption that whenever there is a deficit in the balance of payments—such a balance being defined as indicated above— the volume of investments necessarily exceeds available savings. It is implicitly assumed in this approach that the consumption spending of a community is a function of its aggregate income and not of its aggregate expenditure. If expenditure rises without any rise in income, there is no reason for consumption to undergo any change. But external disequilibrium is merely the expression of an increase in expenditure in relation to the product, which by definition is equal to the income. Since one cannot conceive of an increase in consumption independent of a prior expansion in income, it is fitting to conclude that an autonomous increment in expenditure

---

11 The price elasticity ratio of external demand must be higher than 1.

does reflect an expansion in investment. And because saving is the difference between income and consumption, whereas investment is the difference between expenditure and consumption, the obvious inference is that whenever expenditure rises above the national product there is bound to be a situation of over-investment—that is, insufficiency of savings. Disequilibrium of this type cannot be corrected by mere devaluation unless the latter leads to permanent redistribution of income in favor of the high income groups, or, to put it another way, in favor of those groups with higher propensity to save. In practice, devaluation causes a distribution of income unfavorable to the wage-earning sectors and may, by promoting savings, eliminate over-investment. Nonetheless, such redistribution is only temporary, for the wage earners tend after a lapse of time to endeavor to recover their previous position. Thus further devaluation is needed if a return to a state of disequilibrium between savings and investment is to be avoided. Such being the case, there will be a need for starting to treat the disequilibrium through a reduction in the volume of investments, that is, by deflationary measures.

The validity of this line of reasoning is merely "formal," for the balance of payments deficit may be used either to finance over-investment or to subsidize consumption. If there is an expansion in investment—even if such investment is financed by inflationary means—there will also be an increase in the product and in income and hence in consumption, which is a function of income. This increase in consumption will call in turn for greater imports, augmenting the balance of payments deficit. If we assume that the point of departure had been a situation of full employment, inflationary investments would not affect real income; their effect would remain limited to an increase in the price level within the country. With a fixed exchange rate, domestic equilibrium will be regained when every increase in monetary income has been transformed into a debit in the balance of payments. The outcome will therefore be a rise in costs and prices, a typical case in which only devaluation can reëstablish the balance of payments equilibrium. In a second hypothesis, it might be supposed that the initial situation is not one of full employment and that a rise in investments brings about an increase in the real product. If importing capacity is not augmented concomitantly and if the exchange rate is fixed, a state of disequilibrium in the balance of payments would develop. Hence there would be an expansion in the real product and an even larger one in aggregate expenditure. In this case, to try to correct the disequilibrium by means of a reduction in the volume of investments would amount to causing a contraction in the real product.

The last-mentioned example brings us back again to the problem of the underdeveloped economies. We have seen in the last chapter that a structural tendency towards a rise in the import coefficient emerges in the intermediate and higher phases of underdevelopment. Any attempt to increase the rate of growth tends to exert pressure on the balance of payments. There are manifold reasons for this phenomenon. Among them we ought to emphasize, as deserving of more thorough analysis, the high density of imports in the composition of investments. The result of these fundamental tendencies is that any policy of development necessarily acquires the external characteristics of an inflationary policy; in order to defend stability, measures detrimental to development are often proposed. Let us take the case of an underdeveloped economy whose capacity to import has been increasing slowly—a common situation during the past three decades. Let us suppose that this economy endeavors to raise its investment coefficient without resorting to any inflationary expansion, by means of adequate fiscal methods. The increase in investment will lead to an increment in the product and income, but a rise in income will require larger imports. If the exchange rate is fixed, a balance of payments deficit will tend to pile up, concealing an increase in consumption exceeding that ascribable to the rise in real income as well as a rise in investments higher than that corresponding to the larger savings. Two separate phenomena are involved here, the real increase in investments and in real product; and an expansion in imports higher than importing capacity can stand, which leads to consumption subsidies and to over-investment. As the latter phenomenon is inflationary and appears simultaneously with the former, it is not always clear that the inflation is not the result of the increase in investments but rather of unsuitable guidance of those investments—that is, insufficient substitution of imports. An erroneous diagnosis may have serious practical consequences, as we shall see.

In the instance mentioned above, in which disequilibrium in the balance of payments does not appear concomitantly with a rise in the price level, the advisable corrective would be immediate devaluation so as to curtail the demand for imports. In the case of an economy in an intermediate phase of underdevelopment, it may be taken for granted that the import coefficient would be much higher in the investment than in the consumption sector. Hence the effects of devaluation on the domestic price level would acquire a far more definite form in the capital goods than in the consumption goods sector. There would thus be an immediate reduction in the real savings of the community, which might wholly frustrate the development policy.

In economies of the type we are considering, any attempt at correcting disequilibrium through devaluation soon leads to a reduction in the rate of growth for the simple reason that it increases the prices of capital goods in relation to consumption goods prices. Thus a basic incompatibility stands out between the equilibrium in the balance of payments, as obtained by a fluctuating exchange rate or by successive devaluations, and a development policy aimed at an increase of capital formation. As a matter of fact, if readjustment in the exchange rate is not permitted, then the pressure against the balance of payments remains high, and serious administrative and other difficulties may arise. Indeed, this situation has arisen in a number of countries, including Brazil, as a choice between abandonment of the policy of development and multi-plication of administrative measures as a defense against a sharp disequilibrium in the balance of payments, projected upon the structure of costs and prices in the form of manifold distortions. For inflation in this case is not an autonomous phenomenon, but an overt expression of structural maladjust-ments which follow in the wake of the growth process in some phases of underdevelopment; disequilibrium of the balance of payments is similarly a manifestation of structural anomalies. Unless these maladjustments can be foreseen and avoided, the cost of avoiding inflation and external disequilibrium is high: economic stagnation or, at least, a restricted rate of growth.

As suggested in the analysis expounded in the last chapter, when the main dynamic factor is not expansion of exports, the essence of the problem lies in the fact that the structural transformations required by a particular growth rate are of far wider scope in the intermediate and higher stages of underdevelopment than in developed economies. The larger the amount of new investment to be made in fields in which entrepreneurial experience is still lacking (that is, when the structural transformations required for development are of great scope), the more imprecise the price system is as a guiding device for investments. In a highly diversified struc-ture almost all new investment takes place in existing produc-tion lines and is based on expectation derived from the current entrepreneurial experience in each production sector. In this situation it is to be expected that the price system will convey an idea of the relative profitability of each sector, at least as regards the "present moment." Even in a highly developed economy, however, the price system is not able to afford a dependable idea of relative profitability of alternative projects for long-run undertakings. Indeed, the uncertainty surrounding any undertaking which will be yielding a profit in the future is the very essence of the capitalist form of organizing production.

The price system is generally recognized, then, as an imprecise guiding device in the capital formation process. And it was in order to embody that imprecision in their models that economists developed the theory of risk. However, when accumulated entrepreneurial experience broadly covering all the productive sectors is available, then the economic risk can be calculated in satisfactory terms. Empirical experience places at the disposal of the entrepreneur a number of indicators on which to base his expectations. In underdeveloped economies, the problem is different. In many cases the undertaking is a pioneering venture and the entrepreneur has to figure out his expectations on a purely conjectural basis. Thus speculation as to the probable reaction of foreign competitors—the price elasticity of external supply in the sector of his undertaking—becomes a fundamental datum. This entrepreneur knows that in his attempt to substitute imports he will have to face a competitor who has managed as a result of his exceptional qualifications to achieve a place on the international market. Such a competitor has in his hands two powerful weapons. One is a matter of his financial power, which makes it possible for him to uphold his position in the market by lowering prices if need be. The second consists of the possibility of establishing himself in the "competitor-to-be" country, sheltered from tariffs and other protectionist contrivances. Because of the greater technical experience he enjoys as a result of his position in the market, and the prestige attached to his trademarks, etc., the international entrepreneur has obvious competitive advantages. Even if he is not interested in locating a branch of his enterprise in the prospective competitor country, thereby competing with his own export lines, when faced with the loss of those lines he may well be disposed to integrate into another national economy in order to defend his position on the market.

In practice the situation turns out as follows: In view of the relatively slow increase in importing capacity, investments in the sector substituting imports must grow at a rate higher than that of investment in the sectors which have already been producing for the domestic market for some time. The risk involved in such investments is greater, however, and experience in the newer sectors is smaller or even nonexistent. Hence if the resources at the disposal of the entrepreneurs increase, they naturally prefer to intensify their investments in lines already established. This accounts for the permanent over-investment found in sectors such as the textile industry in many underdeveloped countries, including Brazil, and the final result tends to be excess production capacity in some sectors and insufficiency in others, especially those in which imports have to be substituted. It is a case of initially domestic disequilibrium due to inadequate orientation of investments and consequent idle capacity. Hence a phase of acceleration in investments is also a phase of reduction in the output:capital ratio—an increase, in effect, of idle capacity. Internal disequilibrium comes into existence because of insufficiency of supply, which is reflected in pressure on the balance of payments.

Viewed from another angle, the problem is as follows: Any attempt at increasing the investment rate without proper orientation of the new resources invested creates internal disequilibrium between the structure of supply and the composition of demand; this disequilibrium is transferred to the balance of payments if exchange rates are fixed or is reflected in a rise in internal price levels if exchange controls are in force. Elimination of these external or internal disequilibria requires guidance of investments and not necessarily reduction of their total amount, for if their level is reduced equilibrium is regained only at a lower level of economic activity and therefore through a reduction in the rate of growth. If the intention is to further a policy of development, then the level of economic activity should by no means be sacrificed in order to correct the disequilibrium. There is therefore a need for a methodical reorientation of investments in order to reduce the import coefficient. In short, if development policy is to leave stability unharmed, it ought to take the form of positive guidance of the capital formation process. It is not merely a question of creating favorable conditions for entrepreneurs to intensify the investment effort; it is necessary also to make sure that the investments will produce the structural changes required by development. Actually, there is no fundamental reason why development should not proceed at a fast rate and under conditions of relative stability, both internal and external. What we have endeavored to demonstrate is merely the impracticability of such an occurrence—in the intermediate and advanced phases of underdevelopment—without suitable orientation of the capital-formation process.

Index

Accumulation of capital: employment capacity, 7; Malthusian theory, 8; Ricardo's principle of rise of wages and, 8; viewpoint of theory of distribution, 10-11 and n. 12; Smith's theory, 10 and n. 10, 44; viewpoint of reserve of consumption goods, 14; Marx's theory of, 23 ff. and n. 28; and concentration of ownership, 25-26; changes in composition of capital, 26-27; general law of, 29, 31; intensification of, 30; progress of techniques and, 31; theory of stagnation, 39; supply of savings, 40; moral justification of property, 40; in nineteenth century, 42; as source of income, 44, 45; three aspects of, 44; innovations and, 51; organization of production and, 52; distribution and utilization of income and, 52; results in physical productivity of labor, 62; increase in real income initiates, 65; dependent on technological progress, 69; reproducible, 69; and per capita income, 70; production surplus and, 79, 81-82; transformation of, into productive capacity, 80, 82; based on slavery at outset, 80, 81, 86-87; trade and, 80, 84, 89; commercial expansion and, 81, 88

Agricultural economy, family unit, 67

Argentina, high average productivity of capital, 70

Availability of goods and services, 77-78; price and, 78

Banking system: issues script, 46; determines interest rate, 46; controls supply of capital, 46; commercial houses operating as banking houses, 110, 112 n. 4

Berstine, E. M., 155-156

Brazil, 76; monetary character, 133; sectors in economy, 133 ff.; diversification in consumption habits; disequilibrium in balance of payments, 133-134, 140, 148, 150; coffee economy, 134 ff. and n. 11,

145, 147; oversupply and artificial control, 135, 136 n. 12; demand for manufactured goods, 135-136; foodstuffs and textile imports, 150; import coefficient, 151, 154, 159; choice between abandonment of development and administrative measures, 168; inflation, 168; overinvestment in textile industry, 170

Budget, individual: consumption basic in, 41; saving, 41

Business cycles: Marx's theory of cyclical crises, 30-31, 34; secular trend theories, 57-58; mechanism of, 58; countercyclical policy, 58; in free enterprise economy, 66

Capital goods industry: nonreproducible goods, 68-69; reproducible capital, 68, 69; different levels of productivity, 69-70; cyclical fluctuations and, 71; deficiency in utilization, 71; to middle of nineteenth century, 122; economic growth and production capacity of, 122; profits, 123; in England, 124; transfer of labor from consumer goods industry, 124; surplus of supply, 125; technology and, 126

Capitalistic economy: organic composition of capital, 27; Marx's theory of development in, 21, 23, 24-26, 31, 34-35; historic experience, 34; repeated crises and waste of resources, 35; accumulated resources as source of income, 44; entrepreneur and, 44 ff., 131; Schumpeter's emphasis on technological progress in, 47; a phenomenon, 47; capital-output ratio, 59; commercial expansion in, 81; penetration into underdeveloped structures, 129 ff.; stable consumption and, 131

Cassel, Gustave, 36; concept of sacrifice, 40, 41

Central America countries, pre-capitalistic structures, 133

Chile, 75; loses world monopoly of nitrogen, 160; exports of copper, 164

Classic economists: free competition, 4-5; free exchange, 4-5; technical progress replaces manpower by capital, 9-10; residues of feudalism, 13, 57; on capitalism, 13; ideological-revolutionary, 13-14; theory of labor value, 14, 36, 42; theory of prices, 14; capital as "wage fund," 15, 24; saving as a sacrifice, 17; decline in profit, 34; surplus social product, 36; surplus reverts to entrepreneurs and landowners, 36; work and salaried labor, 36; wages, 36-37; tendency toward stagnation, 39

Consumer goods industries: transfer of labor from, to capital goods industries, 124; lower-priced equipment, 125; increased profit level, 125; lower prices, 125

Consumption: in individual's budget, 41; limits to capacity of, 41; consumer expenditure a function of income level, 58; diversification with rise in income, 64; growth in, essential for investment, 74; division of national product between investment and, 75; diversified through trade, 80, 81, 82, 85; basis of commercial activities, 80

Costs, production: increasing significance of, 103; smaller profit margins, 103; in Flemish woolens, 104; production techniques and, 106-108; basic problem of industrial economy, 109

Countercyclical policy, 58-59; merges with stabilization policies into development policy, 58

Cuba: foreign trade and development, 4; integration into international trade, 4; fluctuations in demand for sugar, 4; capital formation, 4; sugar economy, 147

Customs tariffs, 103

Deflation, 164 ff.

Demand: effective, 32 n. 38; development of, 66 ff.; diversification of, with rise in real wages, 67; rate for food, decreases with rise in real income, 67; evolution of, 67; in consumer expenditure and investment, 68; investment and future, 68

Devaluation, 162 ff.

Development, economic: theory of, 1 *et passim;* rise in real income per capita, 6; concern of classicists, 13, 57; basis in accumulation of capital, 40, 52; incentives to investment, 45; population growth in nineteenth century, 55; farm frontier in nineteenth century, 55; mechanism of, 57 ff.; by-product of business-cycle theories, 57-58; countercyclical and stabilization policies, 58; input-output studies, 59; technological knowledge, 61; increase in real social income, 62, 65, 66, 77, 78; changes in structures of demand and of production, 62; result of new combinations of production factors, 62, 64; obstacles, 64; foreign trade, 64-65; rate of, 68 ff.; capital productivity, 68; capital accumulation, 69; ratio of investment to income, 71; psychological motives of investor and consumer, 72; specific problems, 74; division of national product between consumption and investment, 75; historic process, 77 ff.; dynamics of price system, 77; production surplus, 78, 79; process in pre-industrial countries, 81; uneven process, 83-84; transfer of resources, 84

Disequilibrium, external: in balance of payments, 133-134, 140, 148, 157, 159, 162, 165, 166-168; monetary analysis of, 154 ff.; criterion of normality, 156; cyclical fluctuations, 156; reduction in value of exports, 157, 159; inflation, 157-158, 159; persistent, 159; consequences of devaluation, 162-164; direct deflation, 164

Diversification: basis of commercial activities, 80; of consumption through trade, 80

Domar, E. R., 59

Duesenberry, James S., 72

Employment: capacity of economy, 7; full, requires profitable investment level, 58; spontaneous equilibrium with level of full, 53; cyclical fluctuations in level of, 72

England: farming 1849-1859, 32; industrialization, 43, 125; free imports of farm products, 43; in eighteenth century, 83; prohibits import of textiles, 103; English vessels, 103; protectionistic policy of fourteenth century, 103; later free-trade policy, 103; capital exports, 124; Victorian imperialism, 124

Entrepreneur: theory of, 44 ff.; "salary" of, 45; anticipates profit, 46, 47, 49; creative action, 47; innovations in production process, 47, 51-52; credit system and, 47; Schumpeter's view of, 47, 49-50; reduces costs, 50; new techniques or combinations, 50; production schedules and market predictions, 54; knows cost curves, 54

Equilibrium: theory of general, 36; neo-classicist view of, 39; rate of interest establishes, between savings and demand for capital, 39; Marshall's tendency toward, 48-49; Schumpeter's theory of non-existence of, 48; with level of full employment, 53

Expansion: technological, 127-128; displacement of frontiers, 128, and role of gold, 132; in pre-capitalistic population regions, 129

Factories, rise of, 104, 106; resistance by guilds, 104; competition, 104, 106; costs, 105, 106; payroll, 105

Farming techniques, progress in: urban development and, 90; trade, 96-97; mechanization and the labor market, 126

Feudalism: closed economy, 90, 101; high level of consumption, 90; local resources, 91; surplus production, 91, 96; regressive social organization, 91; construction, 92; retinues, 92; obstacles to unification, 93; land-holding group, 101

Free enterprise economy: "free exchange," 4; "free competition," 4; cyclical fluctuations inherent in, 66, 71; process of development through investor, 72; coefficient of investment in, 73-74; ceiling on investment, 74; produces own market, 74; differences from planned economy, 74 n. 10; investment of income, 113; capital formation, 113; instability of, 113-114

Greek city-state: tribute, 88, 89; slavery, 88; commercial profit, 88, 89; political instability, 88, 95

Guilds, 99-100; resist factories, 104; final overthrow of, 105

Hansen, Alvin, 52, 55-56; theory of economic maturity, 52; analysis of development, 55

Harrod, R. F., 59

Hegel: philosophy of law, 12-13; influence on Marx, 21

Industrial economy, development: European, 96; transformation from commercial economy, 96; factories, 104-106; investment opportunities, 107; sales prices, 108; organization and production techniques, 108; growth and instability, 109 ff.; development in depth, 109, 120; profit residual, 111; contrast with commercial economy, 111-112; price elasticity of demand, 118; revolution in supply and decline in prices, 118-119; demand for capital goods, 119; consumer goods, 120; technical innovations, 121; wages, 121; elasticity of labor supply, 123-124; disequilibrium between producing and absorbing capital goods, 124

Industrial Revolution, 12, 116, 118, 120

Innovation, theory of, 50-52

Input-output studies, significance of, 59

Income flow: distribution of, 31; real, per capita and capital accumulation, 70; fluctuations, 78; increase in productive capacity, and, 78

Interest rate: in neo-classic model, 39; creates savings, 39; result of reduction in, 40-41; nineteenth-century high, 42; determined by banking system, 46; and investment, 55

International Monetary Fund, 160

Investment: for profit, 39, 55; in nineteenth century, 42, 55; incentives to, 45; theory of, 53; Keynes' theory, 53, 55, 59-60; influences demand, 54; interest rate and, 55; technical progress and, 55-56; age pyramid and less opportunity for, 55; toward productivity of capital, 56 and n. 55, 60; new land as, 69; "planned," 58; income-generating factor, 60; reinvestment, 66; development of demand, 66; coefficient of, 71; psychological motivations of saver, 72; free enterprise economy produces own market for, 74; growth in consumption requirement for, 74; determined by rate of investment and average productivity of capital, 74; division of national product between consumption and, 75; factors determining, 75; defined as difference between expenditure and consumption, 165

Italian cities: mercantile bourgeoisie, 94; Venice, 94-95; entrepôts, 94

Japan: high average capital intensity, 70; low per capita income, 143

Kaldor, Nicholas, 115 n. 1, 122 n. 8

Keynes: theory of investment, 53, 55, 59-60; full employment, 53-54; unemployment, 54; fluctuations in level of income, 59; conditions of dynamic equilibrium, 59-60; investment as income-generating, 60; as capacity-generating factor, 60; psychological motives of saver and investor, 72

Labor: Marx's theory of use-value and exchange value, 15; dichotomy between, and labor force, 16; sole production factor, 16; replacement of, by capital, 36; theory of labor value basis of Marx's *Capital*, 36; elasticity of, 128

Laissez-faire regime: competition, 98; profit margins, 99; in foreign trade, 99

Malthus: population principle, 8, 29; law of diminishing returns, 8
Marshall, Alfred, 39, 40, 41; concept of waiting, 40; theory of general equilibrium, 47-48
Marx, Karl: model, 11-14; philosophy of history, 12, 14, 24; influence, 12; problem of production relations in capitalist regime, 13, 14, 19, 21; economic thinking, 13; on capitalism, 13-14; utopian-revolutionary, 14; theory of surplus value, 14, 15, 16, 24, 25-27, 33-34; labor concept, 15-16, 18-19; 36; ignores time factor in production process, 17; saving and monopoly, 17; price theory, 19; doctrine of class struggle, 19, 26; value of social product, 20 ff.; profit rate, 20; "degree of exploitation," 20; theory of capitalistic accumulation, 21, 23, 24-26, 31; production and consumption goods, 22 ff.; stability of real wages, 27-28; progress of techniques, 28, 31-32; unemployment, 28-29, 33; temporary nature of capitalism, 30-31; concept of industrial reserve army, 33-34; influence, 35
Mercantile economy, growth in: profit motive, 85, 86; expands economic universe, 85, 86; low level of productivity, 86, 96; trade, 89, 93-94; along Italian coast, 93; Venice, 94; speedy development, 95; craftsmanship production, 97; rules and regulations, 98-99; guilds, 99; level of income and profits of commercial class, 109; banking houses, 110; stationary, 110, 113
Middlemen, 81
Mill, J. S.: theory of economic progress, 9; ignores technical advancement, 11, 31-32; profit threatened by rising costs of manpower, 11, 29, 31
Myrdal, Gunnar, 14, 45 n. 44

Neo-classic economists: supply of labor and employment, 37, 38, 53; optimistic expectancies, 37; decline in profits in equilibrium, 38, 39, 53; theory of development, 38, 39; on capital accumulation, 38-39; shift from position of equilibrium, 39, 53; no concept of economic progress, 39; rate of interest, 39-40; profit, 39; saving as moral virtue, 41; saving determined autonomously, 41; consumption, 41; contrast with classistic thinking, 42-43; costs of factors, 79. *See also* Keynes

Pirenne, Henry, 93
Polak, J. J., on disequilibrium, 161
Population: idea of surplus, 37; nineteenth-century growth and development, 55; curve in industrial countries, 55
Pre-industrial economies: development process in, 81 ff.; treasure dissipated, 86, 87

Price stabilization policy, 58-59

Production: increased economic productivity, 5-6; theory of, 6; increase in entrepreneur's profits, 5-6; labor-saving factor, 6; development of, forces, 21; level determined by demand, 54; disparities in levels per capita, 69 and accumulation of capital, 62 ff.; increase in real income, 62, 65; increase in demand, 62, 65 ff.; changes in structure of, 62; fluctuations in utilization of capacity; ratio of net investment to net product, 71; surplus, 78-79; 81-82; costs and progressive improvements, 106-108

Productivity of labor: growth in, 1; repercussions on distribution and utilization, 1, 5; division of labor, 7, 10; use of machines, 7, 9; size of market, 7; neo-classic viewpoint, 37, 38; determined by density of capital, 38; capital accumulation and, 38, 62; wages, 40; price mechanism may annul effects of, 67; rise in flow of income, 66; rise in real wages, 66

Profit: rising costs of manpower threaten, 11; rate and speed of turnover of capital, 20; decline in rate of, 30-31; cyclical crises and collapses, 30; participation of wage earners in product reduces, 38; incentive to investment, 45; Schumpeter's theory, 48; expands economic universe, 85, 86; merchant group, 85; cost of production and, 103; in pre-industrial economies, 117, 118

Real wages: no arbitrary level, 7; dependent upon labor supply and employment capacity, 7; Marx's theory of stability of, 27-28; determined by marginal productivity of labor, 38, 66; capital accumulation and rise in, 38; how determined, 38; demand diversified with rise in, 67; lower consumer goods prices and, 125, 126

Research laboratories, 52

Ricardo: theory of rent, 3, 8, 29; study of machines and organization of production, 3; rise of wages and capital accumulation, 8, 9; free agricultural imports, 8; technical progress and price of food, 9, 32; landowners enemies of industrial class, 9; profit threatened by costs of manpower, 11; "economical" techniques, 32; theory of distribution, 43; of comparative costs, 43

Roman empire: slavery and tribute, 86-87, 91; difficulties of transportation and communication, 87; military expansion, 87; commercial development, 87-88; commercial profit, 88; collapse, 89; depopulation, 90

Savings: equilibrium between demand for capital and supply of, 39; capital accumulation and, 40; neo-classicist view of, 41; individual budget and consumption, 41; automatic, 41; by industrial class, 41; psychological motivations, 72

Say, J. B.: elements of production, 7; law, 46; Wicksell overthrows, 46

Schumpeter, J. A.: progress in neo-classic economy, 45; subversion of theory of general equilibrium, 45; creative action of entrepreneur, 47, 49-50; innovations into production process, 47, 51; importance of technological progress, 47; spurious universality, 47; on profit, 48, 50; monopoly, 48, 49; accumulation of new capital, 51

Slavery: accumulation based on, 80; permanent surplus result of system of, 81; intensive usage of labor, 91; replaced by serfdom, 91

Smith, Adam: 6-7; division of labor and productivity, 7, 10, 14; economic progress, 10, 11; stagnation inevitable, 11; theory of prices, 14; redistribution of excessive wealth, 41-42; industrialization, 43; urban life and utilization of social product, 44; theory of accumulation, 44; "propensity to trade," 47; division of labor limited by size of market, 64-65; production increases from division of labor, 105

South American countries: per capita income, 143; increase in productivity, 145; import coefficient, 145-147

Southeast Asia, 131 ff.; British capital in, 131; profit margin, 132-133

Specialization: facilitates concentration of wealth, 81; geographical, 81

Stagnation, theory of, 39

Stationary state, tendency toward, 9

Surplus, production: in pre-industrial communities, 81; with slavery, 81; appropriation of, by minority groups, 81, 82, 86-87; transformed into source of income, 81, 82; warfare, 87

Technical progress, 9, 55-56, 69, 117; replaces manpower with capital, 9-10, 32; shelving of patents, 56; and capital accumulation, 31-32, 69; interdependence with price of labor, 32; due to initiative of capitalist, 32; with availability of resources, 61; rigidity of technical coefficients, 61 and n. 4; new combinations, 62; in capital goods industries, 125-126; in industrialized countries, 127

Textiles, 101-102, 109; for export, 102; profits spent in Genoa, 109; beginning mechanization of, in England, 118; declining prices, 118, 121 n. 7

Trade: in relation to development, 4; type of export economy, 67; imports for consumption needs of minority, 67; diversification of consumption through, 80; utilization of resources possible by, 80; barter, 81; concentration of wealth from, 81; spread of, 93-94; saturation, 102; growing tension, 103

Trade unions, 56

Triffin, Robert, definition of fundamental disequilibrium, 161

Underdeveloped countries: underutilization of production factors in, 61; scarcity of capital, 61; lack of capital goods industry, 62; labor wasted, 61; growth by adaptation of technology, 62; by world trade, 64, 65; underdevelopment defined, 129

Veblen, Thorstein, 71

Walras, Leon: profit vanishes in free competition, 45; "monetary equilibrium," 46
Weber, Max, influence of puritanism on consumer habits, 71
Wicksell, Knut: profit vanishes in free competition, 45; fluctuations in level of prices, 46; overthrows Say's law, 46; interest rate determined by banking system, 46; capital demand and movement of prices, 46

Marybeth
416-822-1480